# Super Firm

*Tough Workouts*

*Fitness, Health & Nutrition* was created by Rebus, Inc. and published by Time-Life Books.

## REBUS, INC.

Publisher: RODNEY FRIEDMAN
Editorial Director: CHARLES L. MEE JR.

Editor: THOMAS DICKEY
Senior Editor: WILLIAM DUNNETT
Text Editor: LINDA EPSTEIN
Associate Editors: MARY CROWLEY, CARL LOWE
Chief of Research: CARNEY W. MIMMS III
Copy Editor: ROBERT HERNANDEZ
Contributing Editors: JACQUELINE DAMIAN, JANE SCHECHTER

Art Director: JUDITH HENRY
Associate Art Director: FRANCINE KASS
Designer: SARA BOWMAN
Still Life and Food Photographer: STEVEN MAYS
Exercise Photographer: ANDREW ECCLES
Photo Stylist: LEAH LOCOCO

Test Kitchen Director: GRACE YOUNG


Time-Life Books Inc. is a wholly owned subsidiary of

## TIME INCORPORATED

Founder: HENRY R. LUCE 1898-1967

Editor-in-Chief: JASON McMANUS
Chairman and Chief Executive Officer: J. RICHARD MUNRO
President and Chief Operating Officer: N.J. NICHOLAS JR.
Editorial Director: RICHARD B. STOLLEY
Executive Vice President, Books: KELSO F. SUTTON
Vice President, Books: PAUL V. McLAUGHLIN

## TIME-LIFE BOOKS INC.

Editor: GEORGE CONSTABLE

Executive Editor: ELLEN PHILLIPS
Director of Design: LOUIS KLEIN
Director of Editorial Resources: PHYLLIS K. WISE
Editorial Board: RUSSELL B. ADAMS JR., DALE M. BROWN, ROBERTA CONLAN, THOMAS H. FLAHERTY, LEE HASSIG, DONIA ANN STEELE, ROSALIND STUBENBERG
Director of Photography and Research: JOHN CONRAD WEISER
Assistant Director of Editorial Resources: ELISE RITTER GIBSON

President: CHRISTOPHER T. LINEN
Chief Operating Officer: JOHN M. FAHEY JR.
Senior Vice Presidents: ROBERT M. DeSENA, JAMES L. MERCER, PAUL R. STEWART
Vice Presidents: STEPHEN L. BAIR, RALPH J. CUOMO, NEAL GOFF, STEPHEN L. GOLDSTEIN, JUANITA T. JAMES, CAROL KAPLAN, SUSAN J. MARUYAMA, ROBERT H. SMITH, JOSEPH J. WARD
Director of Production Services: ROBERT J. PASSANTINO
Supervisor of Quality Control: JAMES KING

FITNESS, HEALTH & NUTRITION

# Super Firm
## *Tough Workouts*

TIME
LIFE
BOOKS

*Time-Life Books, Alexandria, Virginia*

## CONSULTANTS FOR THIS BOOK

William D. McArdle, Ph.D., is a professor in the Department of Health and Physical Education at Queens College of the City University of New York. A Fellow of the American College of Sports Medicine, he is the author of *Exercise Physiology: Energy, Nutrition, and Human Performance; Getting in Shape* and *Nutrition, Weight Control, and Exercise.*

Robert Panariello, M.S., a registered physical therapist, certified athletic trainer, and certified strength and conditioning specialist, is a senior physical therapist at the Sportsmedicine Performance and Research Center, Hospital for Special Surgery, in New York City. He is also the strength and conditioning coordinator for the St. John's University basketball team, and has served as an athletic trainer at the Olympic Training Center in Lake Placid, New York.

Ann Piccarillo is the owner and director of Manhattan Body, Inc., an exercise studio in New York City. She is a member of the Reebok Advisory Board and is certified by the Aerobics and Fitness Association of America.

Bonnie Bennett Stauffer, Ed.D., is the Director of Upperclass Physical Education at the United States Military Academy at West Point, New York, and serves as an instructor in the Master Fitness Trainer Program for the United States Army. Stauffer has also served as the sports psychologist for the Canadian National Wrestling Team.

*Nutritional Consultants*

Ann Grandjean, Ed.D., is Associate Director of the Swanson Center for Nutrition, Omaha, Neb.; chief nutrition consultant to the U.S. Olympic Committee; and an instructor in the Sports Medicine Program, Orthopedic Surgery Department, University of Nebraska Medical Center.

Myron Winick, M.D., is the R.R. Williams Professor of Nutrition, Professor of Pediatrics, Director of the Institute of Human Nutrition, and Director of the Center for Nutrition, Genetics and Human Development at Columbia University College of Physicians and Surgeons. He has served on the Food and Nutrition Board of the National Academy of Sciences and is the author of many books, including *Your Personalized Health Profile.*

For information about any Time-Life book please call 1-800-621-7026, or write:
Reader Information
Time-Life Customer Service
P.O. Box C-32068
Richmond, Virginia 23261-2068

Library of Congress Cataloging-in-Publication Data
Super firm: tough workouts.
    p. cm. — (Fitness, health & nutrition; v.18)
    Includes index.
    ISBN 0-8094-6134-X. —
    ISBN 0-8094-6135-8 (lib. bdg.)
    1. Exercise. 2. Muscle strength. 3. Circuit training. I. Time-Life Books. II. Series: Fitness, health, and nutrition; vol. 18.
    GV481.S83   1989                    89-4686
    613.7'1—dc19                        CIP

Some of the exercises in this book are advanced and should not be attempted by anyone who is not already physically fit. This book is not intended as a substitute for the advice of a physician or an athletic coach. Readers who have or suspect they may have specific medical problems should consult a physician before beginning any program of strenuous physical exercise.

# CONTENTS

# CHAPTER ONE

# Working Harder

*How to vary your exercise program
to enhance strength, power and
muscle tone*

I f building firm, well-toned muscles is your principal goal in exercising, it is not as if your selection of exercises is limited. There are dozens of different routines that can strengthen your muscles and help you mold a pleasingly contoured physique. Yet even well-conditioned people let their exercise programs lapse at times for a simple reason: Performing the same routines again and again can become monotonous, and you arrive at a point where your level of fitness reaches a plateau and you no longer see much physical improvement.

This book is designed to revitalize your exercise program by presenting a series of harder-than-average workouts that have been designed to require little or no equipment, and — as this chapter explains — that offer quite distinctive ways of taxing or overloading your muscles. Some are advanced variations on familiar muscle-strengthening calisthenic routines; others show new ways to sequence exercises in a manner that makes the total workout more demanding to perform; and, finally, there are techniques for developing power, an aspect of fitness related to muscle strength and tone.

### What gives muscles firmness and shape?

Truly firm muscles have both strength, which involves the maximum exertion of a single contraction, and endurance, or the ability to perform repeated contractions. These two elements of muscular fitness are interrelated: A football player needs muscular endurance to run the length of the field; he also needs power to perform the single, explosive effort to kick or throw a ball. The only way to build muscular strength and endurance is to force the muscles to bear some kind of load, which is called resistance. This resistance can take the form of free weights or weight machines, or you can lift the the weight of your body, as in a push-up or sit-up.

Both lifting your body weight and exercising with an external load stress your muscles in an identical way, causing them to contract and begin a complex series of chemical reactions. This results in changes in the enzymes responsible for fat metabolism, and in the number and size of mitochondria — the cell structures responsible for the release of energy and numerous other improvements. The more you exercise your muscles at or near maximum capacity, the more they adapt. They grow in strength, and to some degree in size as well, with this kind of training.

### Can calisthenics that do not use weights provide a sufficiently strenuous workout?

Calisthenics affect not just the primary muscle groups they target, but also the muscles that assist the movement by stabilizing the body. In a push-up exercise, for example, the up-and-down motion works your arms, chest and shoulders directly. However, your abdominals, thighs, hip flexors, back muscles and buttocks are also given a workout, if less intensely, by their role in keeping the body rigid during the movement. Physiologists call this secondary level of toning muscle co-contraction. By contrast, weight training — especially with machines — tends to pinpoint individual muscle groups, and there is less co-contraction by assisting muscles.

### Do exercises that rely solely on your body weight allow you to adjust the resistance?

Weight training does offer one major advantage over calisthenics. Because weight can easily be added to or subtracted from the load, it is easier to regulate the resistance you are working with precisely, and to increase it as you progress. The incremental progression of the load is a fundamental training method called progressive resistance. This concept is based on physiological research showing that to build strength, you must keep the resistance high and the number of repetitions low — simply adding reps will build local muscular endurance but not strength. In effect, if you can easily perform an exercise more

EASY

MEDIUM

HARD

- ● Center of gravity
- ● Axis of movement

## Making an Exercise Harder

As you grow stronger and your muscles get accustomed to working out, the initial exercises in your strength-training program will become too easy: They no longer provide enough resistance for your muscles to contract against, and if you do not increase the weight, your strength gains will start to level off. The key to increasing the load lies in the mechanics of movement, as shown in the illustrations.

In the sit-up, for example, you move your torso from the hips (the axis of movement). The weight of your torso (applied through the center of gravity) resists this movement. If you can add more weight at this point, the resistance will be greater — and the exercise will therefore be more difficult.

The sit-up shown at top, with your arms extended at your sides, is the easiest to perform because the center of gravity is fairly low in your chest. The result is less weight to hoist. By placing your arms on your chest (*middle*), or behind your head (*bottom*), you move the center of gravity upward. This means you must lift and lower more weight, as suggested by the increasing size of the triangles in the illustrations, effectively creating additional overload.

than 10 times in succession, you must increase the load in order to best achieve additional strength gains.

Although you cannot control resistance as rigorously when relying on your body weight, the load of an exercise can nevertheless be adjusted by variations in the way the movement is performed. By changing the angle of your body position or by shifting your center of gravity, you advance to increasingly more difficult versions of standard exercises, as shown in the illustration on page 9. For example, by performing one of the toughest push-up variations — the scapular shrug, with your torso suspended between two chairs — you greatly increase the load on your upper body muscles. Chapter Two focuses on this concept, offering exercise variations of increasing difficulty that will progressively improve your muscle strength and endurance as you become better conditioned.

Another way of adjusting the amount of stress you place on your muscles while exercising is regulating the pace at which you perform your workout — a technique that is the basis of the circuit-training routines in Chapter Four.

## What is circuit training?
Developed in Great Britain, circuit training involves moving rapidly through a series of 15 to 20 exercises, or stations, targeting different body parts. The idea is to perform the activities consecutively, completing a given number of repetitions at each station but taking very little rest time between exercises. The vigorous pace serves two functions: It can be an effective way to achieve an overload effect, and it can also produce some aerobic, or cardiovascular, benefits along with firming and toning the specific muscles. This book presents a circuit-training routine adapted from a program used at the United States Military Academy at West Point.

## Does strength training also increase muscle power?
Technically, physiologists view muscle power as a subcomponent of strength that defines quick movements in which you propel your body weight upward or forward in short, "explosive" bursts of energy. The vertical jump and standing broad jump, for example, are both high-power activities. Since the force capacity of muscles in slow movements, such as calisthenics, gives some indication of force in quick action, strong muscles will generally be powerful as well. However, it is possible to supplement your training program with routines designed to build explosive power, in addition to speed.

## What is the best way to build power?
A relatively new form of exercise called plyometrics, which involves drills such as jumping, hopping and bounding, is being used by many professional athletes, including basketball and football players, tennis and squash players, divers, volleyball players, sprinters and others whose sports require short, intense bursts of activity. Plyometric

## How Plyometrics Improves Performance

**Gain in vertical jump**

6%
Control group

12.5%
Plyometrics group

The bounding and jumping drills in plyometrics are used by many sports teams to build a type of strength that is ignored by most training programs: "explosive" power. In one study of varsity basketball players, the group that added plyometrics to its training regimens showed a far more significant increase in vertical jump heights than the control group, as shown above.

movements rapidly force the muscles into two types of contractions consecutively: eccentric (lengthening against resistance) and concentric (shortening). The theory is that during the eccentric phase — for example, when you land from a jump — the combination of body weight and gravity creates a forceful contraction that loads your muscles with elastic energy. Then in the concentric phase — when you propel yourself into another jump, for instance — this energy is released in a powerful burst of kinetic (moving) energy, in much the same way as a rubber band shoots forward when released after being stretched. Athletes are reporting success in building explosive power with plyometric drills. Chapter Three offers a complete plyometrics routine designed to condition you for high-power sports.

### What happens if you stop training?

Just as muscles can always be developed, no matter how old you are, they can also deteriorate, regardless of your condition. Detraining — a loss in the ability to function — occurs in all skeletal muscles that are used less intensely than usual. If you must wear a cast on your leg, for example, your calf muscle will begin to become weaker and smaller, and you will have to exercise it specifically when your cast is removed to restore it to its normal appearance and capacity for work. Therefore, even if you are well conditioned, and you stop your workout program completely, your muscle tone will disappear in approximately five to 10 weeks. In fact, former athletes who have not adopted exercise programs are often in worse condition than nonathletes who play amateur sports consistently several times a week.

So even if your muscles are extremely firm and well conditioned, you must continue to exercise in order to maintain your strength and endurance, just as you must continue to perform an aerobic workout to maintain your cardiovascular fitness. The exercises in this book will help you not only to maintain your level of development, but they will allow you to enhance it as well.

### Will you reach a plateau in any long-term exercise program?

Typically, the most noticeable physical improvements in any type of conditioning program occur at the beginning, during the first few months. After that, your body continues to make incremental adaptations that are far less dramatic than your initial gains. At each stage, achieving additional development requires increasing your level of effort. After a while, you will arrive at a point where you are in good shape, and to keep pushing may not be possible — or may even result in an injury. Only you can determine your individual goals in an exercise program and the appropriate time to ease off a bit and perform a routine that maintains your physical condition. The self-assessment tests on pages 12 to 13 will give you an idea of your current level of muscular fitness; the guidelines in the following chapters will help you determine the optimal exercises for you and the approximate length of your workout.

# Sizing Yourself Up

The exercises in this book will help make your muscles very firm, whether you choose classic calisthenics (Chapter Two), a circuit-training program (Chapter Four) or plyometric drills to build explosive power and enhance athletic performance (Chapter Three). Before you plunge into your exercise program, take a few moments to assess your current level of strength.

The exercises opposite will give you an indication of the strengths and weaknesses of your body. This knowledge will help you decide which exercise variations to include in your workout from those given in the following chapters. Jot down the number of repetitions you are able to perform in the four self-assessment tests and retest yourself every month or so to measure your improvement. This can be a powerful tool for self-motivation — and it can be very satisfying to see your muscle strength progress.

Whichever type of routine you design for yourself, precede it with a five- to 10-minute warm-up period and follow it with another five- to 10-minute cool-down. The warm-up prepares your muscles and joints for exertion by increasing the blood flow and warming the tissues. This makes them less susceptible to strains and pulls. The cool-down helps speed recovery by removing lactic acid, a metabolic by-product that can cause pain or soreness if it accumulates in the muscles and bloodstream.

For best results, you should exercise three to five times a week and supplement your muscle routines with an aerobic workout three times a week. The aerobic activity, such as running, biking, swimming or circuit training will build cardiovascular endurance, which — along with muscle strength — is the foundation of overall fitness.

To prevent fatigue, organize your workouts so that each muscle group gets a rest period between exercises. For instance, if you are doing two types of exercises to strengthen your abdominals, alternate them with movements for other body parts. Also, exercise the more easily fatigued muscles last: If you are weakest in the upper body, for example, save your push-up sets for the end of your workout routine.

The tests should be scored as follows: Sit-ups: *Excellent* — 50; *Good* — 40; *Fair* — 30; Knee dips: *Excellent* — 20; *Good* — 15; *Fair* — 10; Push-ups: *Excellent* — 20; *Good* — 15; *Fair* — 10; Squat thrusts: *Excellent* — 10; *Good* — 8; *Fair* — 5.

Measure abdominal strength with this sit-up variation, with chin to chest and arms clasped behind your head *(above)*. Take care not to overarch your back.

To assess thigh strength, slowly lower yourself on one knee with the other leg extended. Use a chair, or hold a partner's hand, for support *(above)*.

The push-up will test your upper body. Since women often have trouble with the classic version *(above)*, they can do the modified, bent-knee form *(top)*.

For arms and shoulders, squat with your weight balanced over your hands *(above left)*. Thrust your legs out behind you *(left)*, then return to the squat.

# Myths of Power Eating

Are there foods that can make you stronger and more powerful or enhance your endurance? Many people believe that certain special substances — ranging from bee pollen to wheat germ — have almost magical powers. And for many years, athletes, trainers and even some scientists attributed strength-building properties to protein and recommended a diet high in protein and low in carbohydrates.

In fact, as the chart on pages 16-17 shows, foods that supposedly increase strength and physical performance have never been shown to accomplish this. Most of these foods do not fulfill any dietary requirements, and those that do are needed in relatively small amounts.

This is true even of protein. While muscle is made of protein, your need for it, even when you undertake a strenuous exercise program, is no greater than that in any well-balanced diet — a daily maximum of 12 to 15 percent of your calories. Most often, foods that are relatively high in protein are also high in fat, a nutrient Americans tend to get too much of. The chart on the opposite page shows the relative percentage of fat and carbohydrates accompanying high-protein foods.

The list that follows details some common myths about protein.

*Extra protein supplies additional energy, increases muscle mass and enhances athletic performance.*

There is no evidence that increasing your protein intake above the Recommended Daily Allowance will provide you with more energy, give you bigger and stronger muscles or improve your athletic performance. Nor do athletes require any more protein than their sedentary counterparts. Using your muscles does not cause them to deteriorate, so no extra protein is required to rebuild them.

Unlike carbohydrates and fat, protein has a minor role as an energy source; it is used only when you exhaust your carbohydrate stores and easily mobilized fat reserves. Even then, protein is an inefficient fuel.

*Taking protein supplements is a good way to increase your overall protein intake.*

Protein supplements are harder to digest than protein-rich food, and when used as a replacement, they are potentially dangerous. They can cause severe dehydration and overwork your liver and kidneys. Excess protein also increases your excretion of the mineral calcium, which can cause bone loss and fractures.

*Taking amino acid supplements will enhance performance and increase muscle mass.*

Amino acids are the building blocks of protein, but taking supplements will not enhance athletic performance or build bigger muscles. Like protein supplements, they can cause health problems. Excessive intake of individual amino acids may cause calcium loss, gout, metabolic disorders, dehydration and kidney strain. Moreover, taking single amino acid supplements can interfere with the absorption of other essential amino acids.

# What You Get with Protein

| Food | | Serving size | Calories | Percent of calories | | |
|------|--|--------------|----------|---------------------|--|--|
| | | | | Protein | Fat | Carbohydrates |
| **Bacon** | | 3 slices cooked | 128 | 15 | 85 | 0 |
| **Beef** | T-bone steak | 3 ounces cooked | 330 | 26 | 74 | 0 |
| **Bologna** | | 3 slices | 195 | 16 | 83 | 1 |
| **Bread** | whole-wheat | 1 slice | 60 | 12 | 15 | 73 |
| **Cheese** | Cheddar | 1 ounce | 115 | 25 | 74 | 1 |
| | cottage, 4% milkfat | ½ cup | 120 | 49 | 40 | 11 |
| **Chicken** | white meat, without skin | 3 ounces cooked | 140 | 81 | 19 | 0 |
| | with skin | 3 ounces cooked | 168 | 63 | 37 | 0 |
| **Egg** | | 1 medium | 80 | 32 | 65 | 3 |
| **Flounder** | | 3 ounces cooked | 58 | 89 | 11 | 0 |
| **Frankfurter** | | 1 medium | 170 | 16 | 82 | 2 |
| **Hamburger** | | 3 ounces cooked | 243 | 36 | 64 | 0 |
| **Kidney beans** | | ½ cup cooked | 105 | 27 | 3 | 70 |
| **Lentils** | | ½ cup cooked | 105 | 30 | 3 | 67 |
| **Milk** | skim | 1 cup | 86 | 39 | 5 | 56 |
| | whole | 1 cup | 150 | 21 | 49 | 30 |
| **Oatmeal** | | 1 cup cooked | 130 | 16 | 15 | 69 |
| **Peanut butter** | | 2 tablespoons | 190 | 16 | 71 | 13 |
| **Pizza** | cheese | 2-ounce slice | 145 | 15 | 25 | 60 |
| **Potato** | baked | 1 medium | 216 | 8 | 1 | 91 |
| **Rice** | brown | 1 cup cooked | 225 | 8 | 5 | 87 |
| **Soybeans** | | ½ cup cooked | 130 | 36 | 43 | 21 |
| **Spaghetti** | | 1 cup cooked | 155 | 13 | 3 | 84 |
| **Tuna** | oil-packed, drained | 3.5 ounces | 207 | 61 | 39 | 0 |
| | water-packed | 3.5 ounces | 110 | 94 | 6 | 0 |
| **Yogurt** | plain, lowfat | 1 cup | 145 | 33 | 22 | 45 |

## The Facts about "Power" Foods

Among body builders and athletes, certain foods have acquired mythical reputations for building power and improving performance. As this chart shows, most of these foods contain no significant nutrients, and none of them has been shown to have any enhancing effect on athletic performance, appearance or health.

| FOOD | CLAIM | COMMENT |
|------|-------|---------|
| Bee pollen | Enhances performance by increasing energy, strength and stamina | Bee pollen does not possess any energy-producing substances and has failed to benefit exercisers. There is no research to support the claim that bee pollen enhances performance. Highly allergenic. |
| Brewer's yeast | Enhances performance | Although this product contains some B vitamins, it has not been shown to improve athletic performance or boost energy levels. |
| $B_{15}$ (Pangamic acid) | Increases the delivery of oxygen to the cells and tissues | $B_{15}$ does not improve oxygen delivery. No evidence exists to show a vitamin function for this substance. Tablets from one manufacturer were found to contain only pure lactose (milk sugar). |
| Caffeine | Supplies energy | Caffeine appears to have no beneficial effect on short-term, anaerobic exercise. Several studies contend that caffeine may improve performance in endurance activities requiring more than an hour of sustained effort. Negative effects include stomach upset, nervousness, increased water loss (due to diuretic properties), dizziness, nausea and headache. |
| Carnitine (Vitamin B-T) | Diminishes muscle fatigue and pain | No evidence has been found to support the claim. There is no dietary requirement for carnitine, so it is not considered a vitamin. |
| Gelatin | Boosts energy, improves endurance | Tests have failed to show any endurance benefit from gelatin or the amino acid glycine found in it. |
| Ginseng root | Boosts energy and sustains endurance | No well-controlled studies have been conducted. Among the problems reported in ginseng users (especially those who have taken large amounts for long periods of time) are nervousness, insomnia, sore breasts, high blood pressure. |

| FOOD | CLAIM | COMMENT |
|---|---|---|
| **Kelp**<br>(Seaweed) | Increases energy, helps bones heal faster; a high-quality protein | Kelp has not been found to increase energy or aid in bone healing. Its protein is of poor quality and minimal. Dried kelp has been found to contain more than eight times as much iodine as iodized salt. |
| **Liver** | Increases endurance, builds strong muscles | Liver is high in iron and protein and is an extremely rich source of retinol, a form of vitamin A. However, liver should not be eaten daily, since a 3.5-oz serving has 354 mg of cholesterol; 300 mg is the daily recommended limit. Liver also raises the concentration of purines (by-products of protein metabolism) in the blood, which may cause gout or kidney stones. |
| **Raw eggs** | High protein content builds muscle mass | Egg protein will not build muscle. Eggs are an excellent complete protein, but the yolk contains a great deal of cholesterol. Do not eat raw eggs; negative effects include nausea, appetite loss, and muscle pain and fatigue (cooked egg white has no harmful effects). |
| **Sodium bicarbonate**<br>(Baking soda) | Increases muscle efficiency; enhances performance; helps reduce muscle fatigue by making blood more alkaline | Most studies, in which subjects have taken between 200-300 mg of baking soda for every 2.2 lbs. of body weight, have failed to link baking soda with improved performance. Can cause diarrhea. |
| **Wheat germ; Octacosanol**<br>(alcohol isolate extracted from wheat germ) | Improves performance, especially endurance; boosts energy | Wheat germ and octacosanol have no known energy-producing effects. |

# CHAPTER TWO

# Advanced Shaping and Toning

*Tough versions of push-ups, sit-ups and other muscle-building calisthenics*

The exercises in this chapter provide a workout that focuses on shaping and toning all of the major muscle groups. Many of the exercises are based on classic calisthenics movements, such as push-ups and sit-ups, but the versions shown here place more of a demand on your muscles and also target them from different angles to enhance their definition. These movements are also excellent for building muscular endurance: One study showed that endurance improved in subjects at the rate of 10 percent per week when they performed 15 to 25 repetitions of an exercise over a period of seven weeks.

The key to getting the most from a calisthenics workout is variety: Firming even one set of muscles requires more than one movement because most exercises not only work specific muscles, but focus on certain portions of a muscle. For example, when you do a traditional sit-up, you are mostly working the upper portion of your abdomen. Your oblique muscles, which taper to define your waist, are hardly exercised at all. By performing the exercises on pages 28-37, you will rotate your torso to work these muscles.

You do not need weights or other elaborate equipment to perform these exercises. A few of them require one or two chairs, but most rely solely on the positioning of your limbs and torso to supply the resistance. The fact that they do not involve weights does not mean they are easy: You need to be in fair condition to perform them properly *(see the self-assessment tests on pages 12-13)*. Even if you are in good shape, you should begin slowly, performing each exercise with the number of repetitions that places a demand on your muscles without straining them.

Because your muscles need time to recover, it is a good idea to alternate exercises for different parts of your body on different days. You will find that your workout capacity will grow faster than if you exercise the same muscles every day, since toning and growth take place during recuperation after you have stressed the muscle. The box at right provides guidelines for using these exercises in a progressive-training program that strengthens muscles by gradually increasing the amount of work they must do.

Using your body weight for resistance requires that you be especially careful to use proper form. For example, it is easy to bend at the waist when doing a push-up, but you will work harder and get more from the exercise if you keep your body aligned correctly and your arms placed properly. For this reason, it is better to do 20 perfect push-ups than 50 push-ups in bad form.

If you cannot complete the suggested number of repetitions (reps), do them in sets. For example, if 20 reps of a negative sit-up are prescribed, perform two sets of 10 or four sets of five with short breaks of 10 to 15 seconds between the sets until you can manage all the reps with no break. Perform the exercises as fast as you can while still maintaining the proper form. You will build more endurance by doing fewer repetitions in quick succession than by doing the full amount slowly.

Pay close attention to your breathing while you perform the exercises. The proper way to breathe is to exhale during the exertion phase of an exercise and inhale during the relaxation phase. Many people unconsciously begin to hold their breath, especially toward the end of a series of repetitions. Researchers have theorized that doing so — in effect, pushing the inhaled air against your chest and throat — may give the illusion of assisting the chest muscles. By pressing on your heart and forcing it to empty blood into the arteries rapidly, the compressed air in your lungs makes your blood pressure rise abruptly. The air also presses on the relatively thin-walled veins leading to the heart, making the return of blood into the heart much slower and causing an abrupt drop in blood pressure. You can become dizzy, see "spots" or even faint. Also, because the heart works hard to pump blood to the muscles when you exercise, it needs more oxygen itself. Restricted blood flow means less oxygen for the heart

# Workout Progressions

If you are not already exercising on a regular schedule, begin by working out three times a week. Do as many repetitions for each exercise as you find comfortable, and then an additional rep for each exercise if possible.

You can train progressively by adding more repetitions to each set of exercises you do. Then increase the total number of sets you perform. Finally, add to the number of days per week that you work out. Do not increase too quickly or you may be injured.

Steadily increasing the number of repetitions and/or sets you perform is an effective way to develop, but it can be boring. An alternative is to train progressively with a sequential plan:

- Week One: Perform the number of sets you can do comfortably for each area of the body in each of your three workout sessions.

- Week Two: Add repetitions in increments of five to each set of exercises.

- Week Three: Add repetitions in increments of five to each set.

- Week Four: Add an additional set with the original number of reps for each exercise.
- Week Five: Repeat Week Two.
- Week Six: Repeat Week Three.
- Week Seven: Repeat Week Four.
- Week Eight: Repeat Week Three.
- Week Nine: Repeat Week Four.

By this time, your training session should take at least 30 minutes. To increase further, add another workout to your training week.

rather than more. In addition, holding your breath during exercise increases intra-abdominal pressure and may even cause a hernia.

Along with breathing steadily and deliberately, it is important to warm up properly before you begin your workout. Warming up increases blood flow to the muscles and the temperature in the muscle core. As a result, your muscles should be able to work faster and more efficiently, and their ability to use oxygen should improve. In addition, warming up should make the blood vessels in the muscles dilate, increasing blood flow to the area, so that oxygen reaches muscle tissue faster and waste products are removed more quickly as well.

Cooling down after exercise is also necessary to remove waste products that accumulate in the muscles as a result of exertion. Stopping abruptly can cause a sudden drop in blood pressure because, when the heart stops pumping hard, the blood can pool in the veins. Good warm-ups and cool-downs are repetitive and aerobic, like running in place, at a moderate level of exertion.

If possible, perform your exercises in front of a full-length mirror, and pay close attention to the line your torso makes and the angle of your legs in the various exercises. Wear tights, a leotard or shorts so that your clothing does not obscure your image.

# The Upper Body

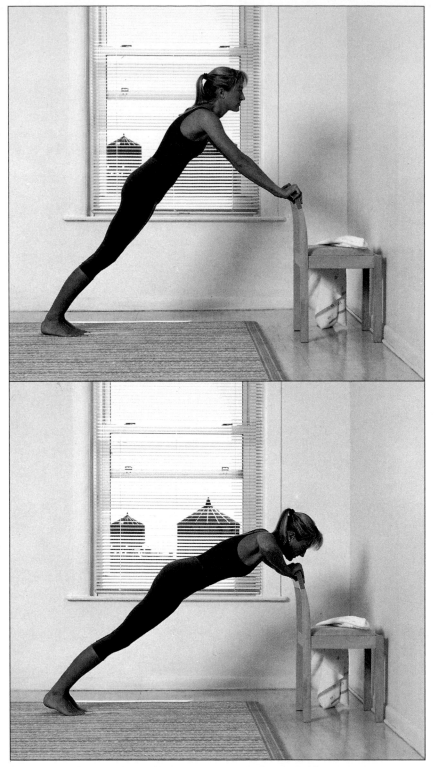

The muscles that can be developed to contribute the most definition to your physique are those of the upper torso and arms — pectorals, deltoids, latissimus dorsi across the middle back and the smaller muscles of the back, biceps and triceps. The fact that these muscles are, in many people, the least exercised body parts means that they often respond quickly to training. Since the upper body generally stores less fat than other body areas, the definition that occurs is more readily apparent.

In the push-ups, hip rotation, hip drop and the scapular shrug, you use your body weight for resistance. The principle to remember when you perform all these exercises is to keep your torso in one plane; do not bend forward at the hip or arch your back.

Focus your gaze at a particular place at about eye level several feet away to keep your head level. This will help you to concentrate on your motion as well. Remember to continue breathing normally as you work out. Perform 15 to 20 repetitions of each exercise.

**Support your aligned body at a 45-degree angle to the floor by holding the back of a chair or other stable piece of furniture** *(top)*. **Without bending at the waist, lower yourself toward the chair** *(above)*. **Return to the starting position.**

To work your deltoids, cross one foot over the other and support your weight with your hands pointed inward *(top)*. Use your abdominal muscles to keep your body rigid as you lower yourself toward the floor *(above)*. If the classic push-up is too difficult, perform the knee push-up *(right)*, making certain to keep your body aligned as you lower and raise yourself.

## Hip Rotation

Assume the push-up position with your feet together and your arms extended at shoulder level (1). Keeping your body rigid, rotate your right hip outward, lifting yourself up onto the fingers of your right hand as you turn (2). Lower yourself to the floor as if for a standard push-up (3). Then raise yourself and rotate your left hip outward, lifting yourself up onto the fingers of your left hand (4). Lower yourself to the floor again (5).

# Hip Drop

With your feet together and your left arm resting at your side, support your aligned body on your extended right arm *(top)*. Bend at the waist to allow your right hip to drop toward the floor *(above)*. Raise yourself again to the starting position.

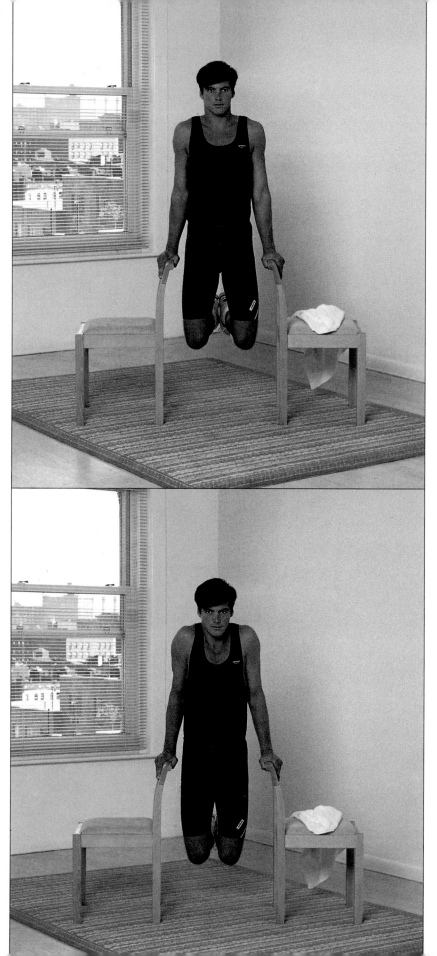

# Scapular Shrug

Support yourself between two stable chairs and bend your knees so that your lower legs are parallel to the floor *(left)*. Then hunch your shoulders, allowing your body to drop lower between the chairs *(below)*. Return to the starting position.

# Double Leg Extension

**2**

**4**

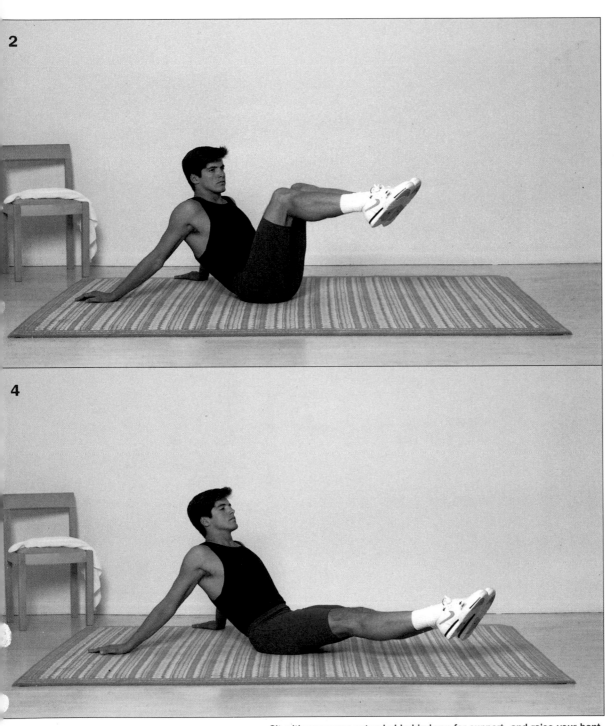

Sit with your arms extended behind you for support, and raise your bent legs off the floor with your feet together (1). Bend your knees and draw them toward your chest (2). Then lift and extend your legs, pointing your toes toward the ceiling (3). Lower your legs almost to the floor, keeping your knees extended but not locked (4).

# Double Leg Raise

**3**

**4**

Sit at the edge of a chair, supporting yourself with your arms bent behind you and holding onto the seat. Extend your legs so your body is at a 45-degree angle to the floor (1). Bend your knees and lift your feet to the height of the seat (2). Then extend your legs and raise them as high as you can (3). Keeping your knees extended, lower your legs to the floor (4).

# Negative Sit-Up

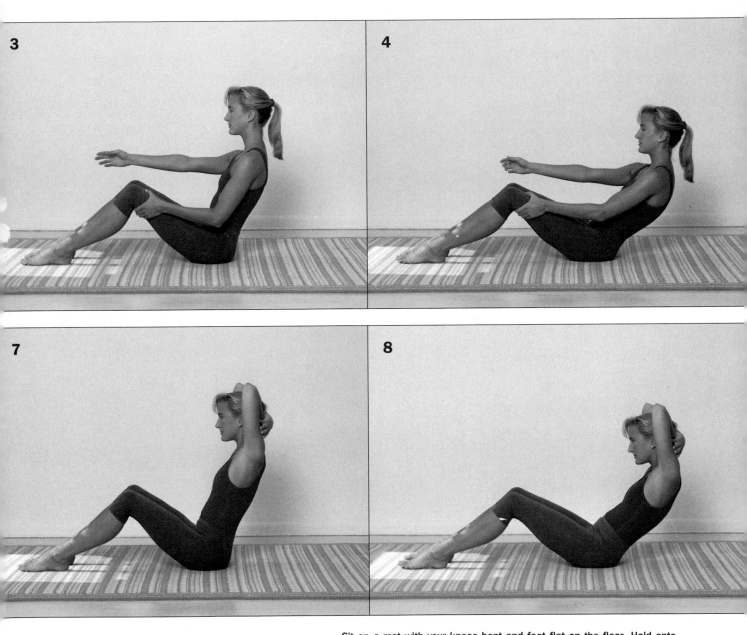

Sit on a mat with your knees bent and feet flat on the floor. Hold onto your thighs close to your knees (1). Round your back as you lower yourself toward the floor to the point where your arms are almost extended (2). Return to the starting position, and reach forward with your right arm (3). Keeping your arm extended, round your back as you lower yourself again, holding your left thigh firmly (4). Repeat steps 3 and 4 with your left arm. Then reach forward with both arms (5), and lower yourself, rounding your back (6). Repeat the sequence with your arms crossed behind your head as shown (7,8).

# Total Body Crunch

Lie on your back with your hands clasped behind your raised head. Draw your right knee toward your left elbow and raise your left leg as high as you can, keeping your knee bent slightly *(above opposite)*. Lower your left leg toward the floor, straightening your knee *(above)*.

Lie on your back with your hands clasped behind your raised head, your thighs perpendicular to your torso and your knees bent *(above opposite)*. Draw your knees to your elbows, keeping your toes pointed *(above)*. Make sure the small of your back is pressed against the mat.

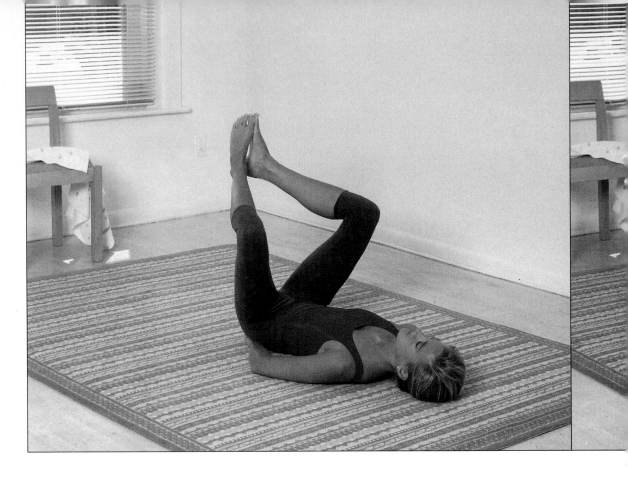

# The Lower Body

Exercises for toning the muscles of the lower body must be especially demanding, since these muscles are often the strongest. Still, toning them is important, particularly the muscles that form the buttocks and those of the inner thigh, since neither of these groups is adequately exercised by everyday activities like walking and carrying groceries.

The exercises that appear on this page and the following five pages are unusual because, if you do them incorrectly, you will find them much too easy. To do them correctly, you must supply resistance by tensing your muscles in isometric contraction while you perform the movement of the exercises.

The exercises on pages 44-47 are especially difficult since they tax the muscles of your back as well as your hamstrings, quadriceps and adductors of your thighs. If you are prone to lower back pain, avoid these exercises. Perform the hamstring-gluteus bend on page 48 to strengthen your thighs and buttocks without stressing your lower back.

The squats and demi-squats on pages 50-53 develop the quadriceps along with the gluteals. Be sure to exhale during the exertion phase of the exercise and inhale during the relaxation phase.

Perform the same exercises on both sides of your body, alternating with each repetition for a total of 15 to 20 reps on each side.

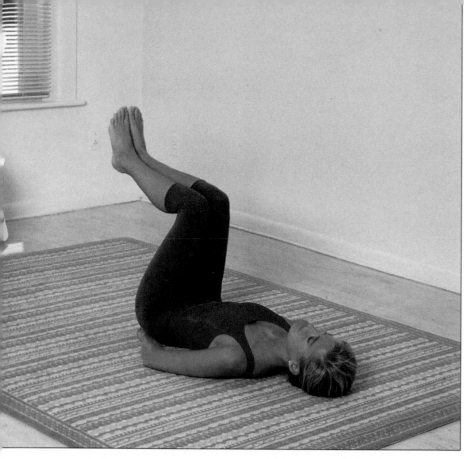

**TRIANGLE PRESS** Lie on your back with your hands placed under your buttocks, feet together and your knees apart *(opposite)*. As you tense the muscles of your inner thighs, press your knees together forcibly *(left)*.

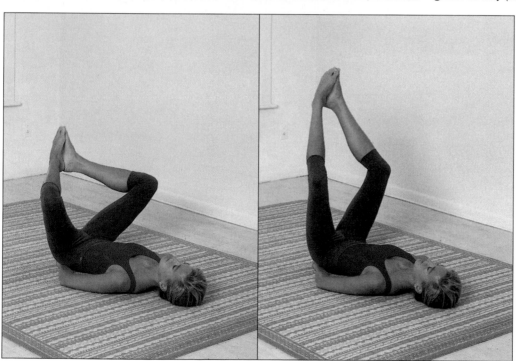

**TRIANGLE LIFT** Lie on your back with your feet together, your knees apart and your hands placed under your buttocks *(left)*. Tense the muscles of your inner thighs as you press your feet toward the ceiling forcibly *(above)*. Return to the starting position.

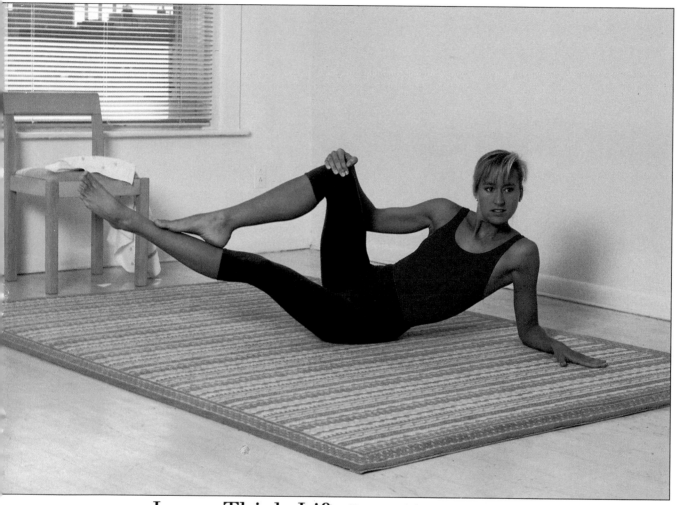

# Inner Thigh Lift

Lie on your left side with your left leg extended and support yourself on your left arm. Hold your bent right knee with your right hand *(opposite)*. Without rotating backward, raise your extended left leg to touch your right foot *(above)*. Return to the starting position.

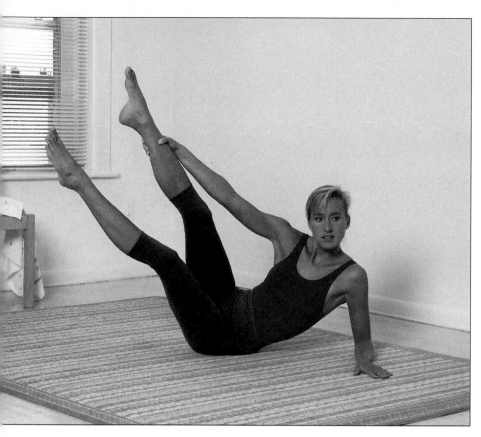

# Hip Balance

Lie on your left side with your left leg extended and hold your extended right leg with your right hand *(opposite)*. Lift your extended left leg toward your right leg *(left)*. Return to the starting position.

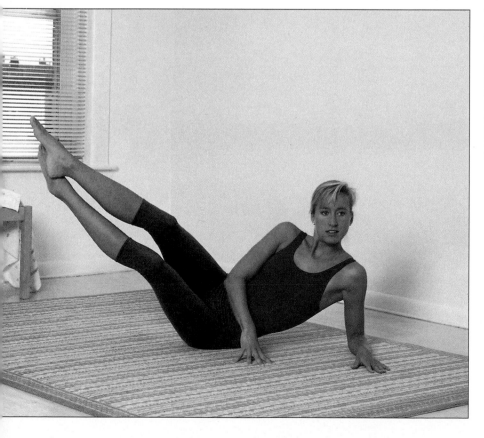

# Diagonal Thigh Lift

Support yourself on your left side with your bent left arm and use your right arm to brace yourself. Raise your extended legs — crossed at the ankles — about a foot off the floor *(opposite)*. Then raise both legs as high as you can without losing your balance *(left)*. Return to the starting position.

# Outer Thigh Lift/1

Position yourself on your knees on a mat with your hands placed shoulder-width apart *(inset opposite)*. Raise your left leg out to the side, keeping your knee bent and your foot parallel to the floor, as high as possible *(inset left)*. Then straighten your knee by bringing your foot forward, so that your extended leg is perpendicular to your torso *(below left)*. Return to the starting position.

# Outer Thigh Lift/2

Balance yourself on your right knee and bent right arm with your left hand and left leg extended behind you *(top)*. Raise your left leg out to the side and behind you *(above)*. Return to the starting position.

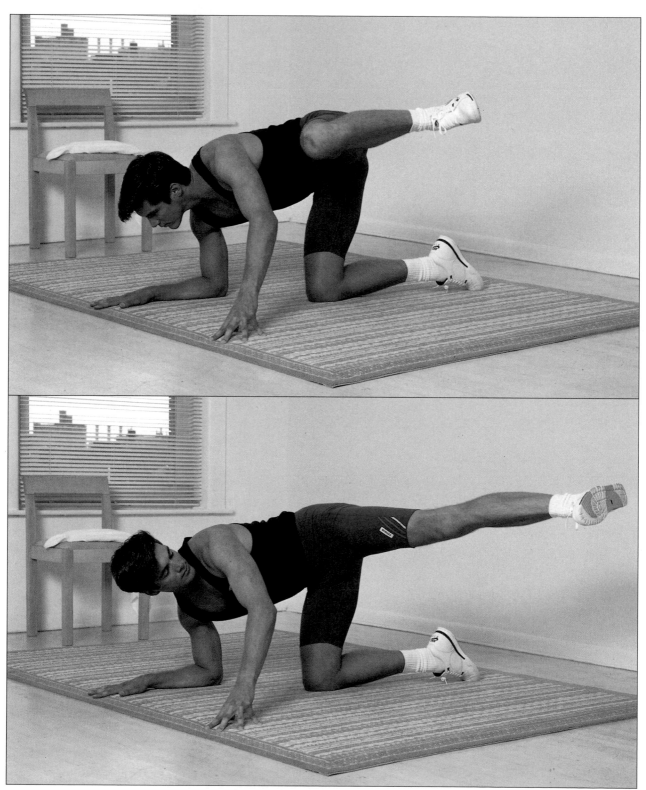

Support yourself on your right knee and bent right arm with your left hand, and raise your bent left leg out to the side *(top)*. Look at your leg as you extend it and flex your foot *(above)*. Return to the starting position.

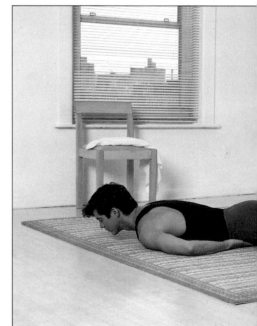

# Hamstring-Gluteus Bend

Lie on your stomach with your hands under your hips, your head resting on your chin and your left leg bent so that your foot is parallel to the floor *(right)*. Raise your left leg off the floor, keeping your knee bent *(opposite)*. Return to the starting position.

# Hamstring Lift

Lie on the floor on your right side, supporting yourself on your bent right arm, and balance with your extended left arm. Hold your extended left leg about six inches from your extended right leg *(opposite)*. Raise your left leg as high as you can *(left)*. Return to the starting position.

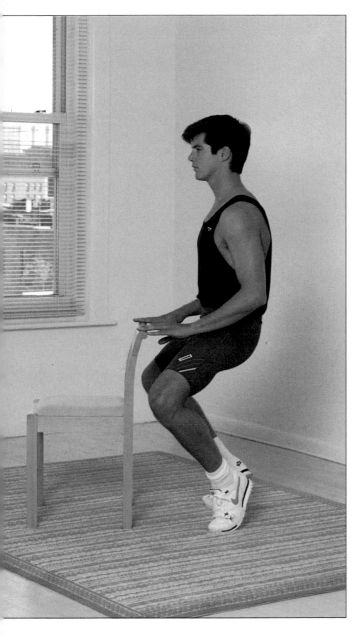

# Demi-Squat

Stand with your feet comfortably apart and your pelvis tucked, facing a chair or other stable piece of furniture with your hands resting on its back *(opposite).* Using the chair to balance, bend your knees outward and rise up on your toes *(center).* Lower yourself until your forearms are parallel to the floor, keeping your pelvis tucked *(left).* Return to the starting position.

# Squat

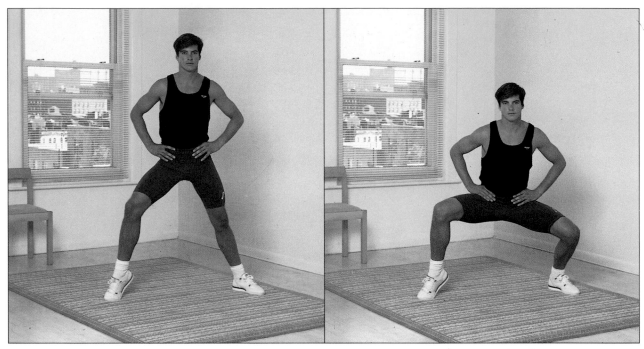

With your hands on your hips and your feet spread apart, stand on your left foot and your right toes *(above left)*. Squat by bending your knees until your thighs are parallel to the floor *(above)*, then stand.

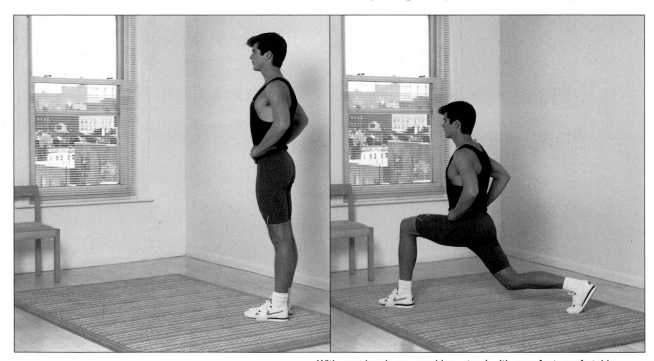

With your hands on your hips, stand with your feet comfortably apart *(above left)*. Squat by lunging forward on your left foot, bending your right knee to the floor *(above)*; then stand erect.

Stand with your feet shoulder-width apart and your hands on your hips *(above left).* Squat by moving your right leg to the side and bending at the waist and knees. Touch your feet with your hands *(above).* Return to the starting position.

CHAPTER THREE

# Plyometrics

*Leaping, bounding and throwing
for explosive bursts of power*

Whatif you could utilize a special reflex to build momentum rather than lose it when you jump, leap or catch and then throw a ball? Or if you could actually increase your power by changing direction when you run or jump? Athletes in Eastern Europe and the Soviet Union discovered a way to do this during the mid-1960s, using an exercise called plyometrics. The power created by plyometrics is usually characterized as "explosive," because it concentrates a large amount of force in a very short period of time. Now Western athletes — football, basketball, baseball and tennis players — are among those who find this training effective, especially in sports that require quick acceleration.

The basis for plyometric exercise is the fact that muscles and tendons are elastic, and so can recoil when stretched. The primary objective of plyometrics is to convert this recoil energy during a muscular contraction into an equal and opposite force. The training to accomplish this involves the rapid stretching of a muscle to produce a

55

forceful movement in a short period of time. This occurs, for example, when you cock your arm to throw a ball, or squat quickly before performimg a vertical jump.

Although each sport requires a different style of plyometric training, depending on the muscles used for the particular activity, the various plyometric movements all utilize three distinct phases: a vigorous stretch, a transition period and a final reaction and motion.

During the first phase, these exercises rapidly stretch the involved muscles. This stretching can occur in the muscles of your legs, for instance, as you land from a jump in place, or you can experience it in the muscles of your arms and shoulders as you prepare to toss a weighted medicine ball.

This first step usually produces a "cocking motion," because your muscles act like coiled springs that store potential energy as they elongate. The crouch you assume just before you jump for a rebound while playing basketball is another example of this action. As you crouch, the muscles in your legs stretch and set in motion a muscular reflex known as the myotatic reflex — a stretch reflex of the muscle spindle. This reflex, which takes place during the first phase of all plyometric activity, activates a powerful neuromuscular stimulus from the spinal cord to the muscles that consequently helps them contract more forcefully than they would without the preparatory cocking motion. That is why the crouch before jumping for a basketball rebound results in a higher leap than standing with your hands in the air before grabbing the ball.

The second phase of a plyometric exercise is the transition between the initial eccentric contraction and the final reaction. Exercise physiologists who have studied plyometrics call this transition the amortization phase. Successful plyometric training focuses on making the amortization phase as brief as possible.

The final phase is the concentric contraction of your muscles, when they tighten and grow shorter. This contraction should take place as quickly as possible, so that the resulting motion is a rapid "explosion" of force.

Because of the swift and intense concentration of force during plyometrics, these exercises should be performed sparingly and with caution. They are not for beginning exercisers or people who are not at least moderately physically fit. You should master the simpler exercises before attempting the more difficult maneuvers. The plyometric exercises shown in this chapter are arranged in order of increasing difficulty for each area of the body.

The more elementary plyometrics *(see pages 59-61)* are the safest and also require the least equipment. These exercises should be performed once or twice a week for four to six weeks before progressing to the more stressful exercises. In particular, strenuous activities, such as in-depth jumps *(see pages 80-82)*, which introduce powerful forces on your knees and tendons, should only be performed if you are able to do a squat with one and a half times your body weight on a

# Equipment for Plyometrics

◆ For running and jumping exercises, you will need a resilient surface at least 25 yards long, such as a wooden gym floor, with adequate space for bounding and leaping. For some exercises, working outdoors on grass is best, either in a large backyard or on a playing field.

◆ To work out indoors, you will need a sizable exercise mat that is dense enough to make jumping safe and comfortable and that will not slide when you land on it.

◆ The plyometrics exercises on pages 78-83 require the use of a raised jumping surface. You can use either a step, bench or a box made of wood and covered with some kind of mat or padding that you can construct or purchase. Depending on your height and your jumping ability, this box should measure eight, 12 or 18 inches on each side for beginners, and it should be sturdy enough to support at least three times your body weight. You may want to use a two-foot box for more advanced training.

◆ For the cone hops on pages 70-73, you will need six-inch rubber cones similar to those used as lane markers on highways. You can find them in sporting goods stores, but you can substitute soft household objects of similar height. These should be sturdy and stable, but soft enough not to cause injury if you fall on them.

◆ A medicine ball is used for the plyometrics movements on pages 84-95. These dense balls were previously made only of leather in the size of a basketball, but now they come in various sizes, and range in weight from three to 16 pounds. They are usually covered with leather or polyurethane. You can find them in sporting goods stores.

barbell across your shoulders, or if you have prepared for these exercises with the previous plyometrics demonstrated in this chapter.

Exercises that require explosive force can injure you if you do not warm up sufficiently. An aerobic warm-up like jogging for five to 10 minutes or cycling on a stationary bicycle should bring the core of your muscles to a safe temperature, and increase the blood supply to your peripheral tissues adequately. And, of course, after your plyometrics workout, you should also take five to 10 minutes to cool down, by performing simple stretches, without bouncing, or a slow aerobic routine similar to a warm-up.

If you train by yourself, without the benefit of a coach or trainer, you should never do plyometrics more than once a week. Do not perform them with ankle, wrist or chest weights, because they increase the chance of injury while decreasing the benefit of the exercise by slowing your reaction time.

For best results, plyometrics should be supplemented with sprint training and weight lifting. Children should not do advanced plyometrics because they are too stressful for their joints; on their own, though, kids often do activities like skipping, bounding and jumping, which are the exercises you should include at the start of your plyometrics program.

# The Lower Body

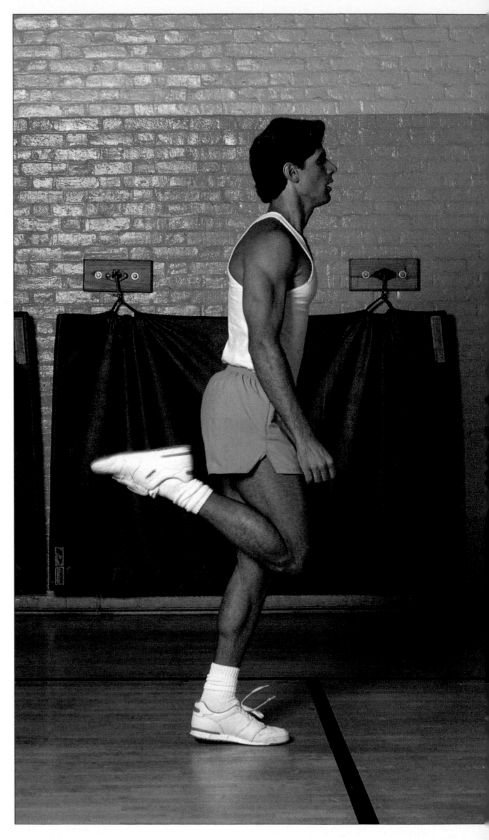

Lower body plyometrics are exercises that develop the legs primarily but, like all plyometric exercises, they require the effort of your upper body as well.

Once you have warmed up sufficiently, perform the exercises in the order given, beginning with the jumps in place, then the standing jumps, multiple hops and bounding. The plyometrics begin in earnest with the cone hops, since these are the first exercises in the sequence that require you to land and then take off immediately.

Your warm-ups can include running in place, as shown on this page, or the hip kicker *(see page 59)* and the split squat walk *(see page 60)*. Always stretch before and after your warm-ups to loosen your muscles.

To perform the cone hops on pages 70-73, you will need six-inch cones made of rubber or plastic that are available in sporting goods stores. Use three cones to begin with, and work your way up to five. You may substitute stuffed toys, or other soft household objects, so long as they are stable and have the necessary height. Be sure not to choose an object you will hurt yourself with should you land on it.

First perform the lead-up exercises shown on pages 58-61, which you can use as warm-ups. Then, for the exercises that follow, begin by performing three sets of five repetitions and work your way up to three sets of 10 reps. The harder the exercise, the fewer reps you should do initially.

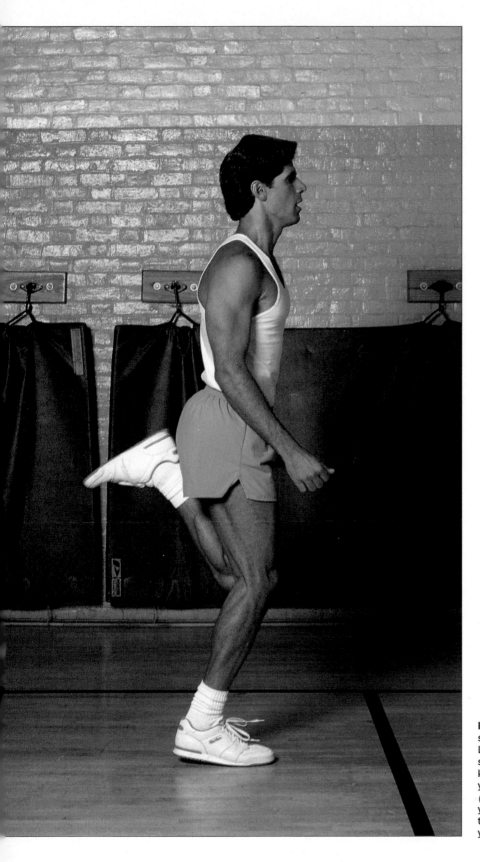

**HIP KICKER** Stand with your arms at your sides and your feet shoulder-width apart. Lean forward slightly with your back straight. Run in place, keeping your knees pointed straight down. Try to kick your right buttock with your right heel *(opposite)*, then your left buttock with your left heel *(left)*. Begin by performing this exercise for 30 seconds, and work your way up to one minute.

# Split Squat Walk

Stand with your hands on your hips and your right leg forward, forming 90-degree angles at the hip and knee, and your left leg extended behind you with your left knee bent (1). Walk forward without raising or leaning your upper body as you progress (2, 3). Complete the stride cycle by regaining the starting position (4, 5). Perform this walk for a distance of about 10 feet at first; increase your distance to 30 feet.

# Double-Leg Tuck Jump

Stand with your feet shoulder-width apart and your arms at your sides (1). Bend forward at the knees and waist with your arms extended behind you (2). Jump straight up, extending your legs, and at the same time swing your arms forward. Then bring your knees up until your thighs are parallel to the floor and grasp your knees briefly with both hands (3). Straighten your legs to land (4).

# Split Squat Jump

Stand with your hands on hips, and, keeping your back straight, lunge your right knee forward to form a right angle and extend your left leg behind you (1). Dip in place so that your knee lifts about six inches from the floor, then launch yourself upward forcefully (2). Land in the starting position (3).

In the Split Squat Jump position (1), dip in place twice about six inches from the floor and then launch yourself upward (2), switching the positions of your legs at the peak of the jump (3). Land in the starting position with your left leg forward (4).

# Squat Jump

Stand with your feet shoulder-width apart and your fingers interlocked behind your head. Squat so that your knees are flexed as shown *(opposite).* Jump straight up as fast as you can *(center).* Land in the starting position *(left).*

# Standing Broad Jump

Stand with your feet shoulder-width apart and your arms at your sides. Bend forward at the waist and knees, as shown, with your arms extended behind you (1). Jump up and forward as far as you can by extending your legs, and swing your arms forward (2). Lift your knees, bringing your feet forward (3), and land with your knees and hips flexed (4).

# Cone Hops

With your feet shoulder-width apart, stand with your arms at your sides and your knees bent slightly *(below)*. Jump up and forward over the first cone by tucking your knees so that your thighs are about parallel to the floor *(center)*. Land with your hips and knees flexed slightly *(right)*. Immediately take off again and jump forward over the second cone. Repeat until you have jumped over all the cones.

# Lateral Cone Hops

Stand to the right of a six-inch cone with your arms extended behind you *(opposite)*. Jump up and sideways over the first cone, tucking your knees so that your thighs are at least parallel to the floor *(center)*. Land with your hips and knees flexed slightly *(above)*. Immediately take off again, jumping sideways over the next cone. Continue until you have jumped over all the cones.

## Power Skipping

From a standing position, step forward with your right leg while swinging your left arm forward (1). Raise your left leg, bending your knee, as you swing your right arm up forcefully, skipping forward into the air (2, 3). Land flat-footed on your left leg and immediately skip upward with your right leg and left arm (4). Try to attain maximum height.

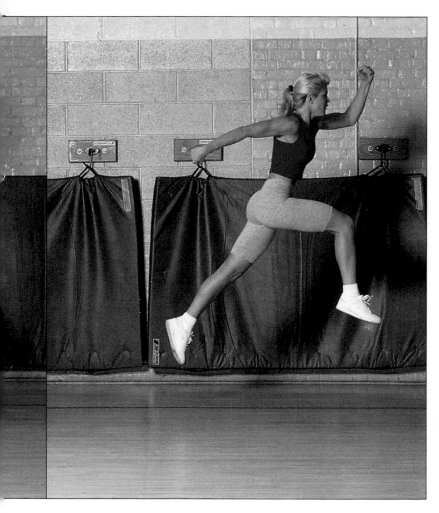

# Bounding

Step forward with your right leg as you swing your left arm forward *(opposite)*. Then leap up and forward by driving your left leg and right arm into the air *(center)*; pretend you are floating. Land flat-footed on your left leg and immediately drive your right leg and left arm forward *(left)*.

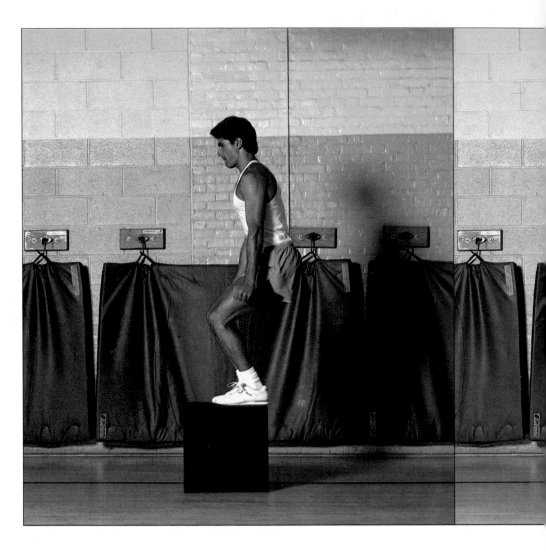

# Box Routines

To build leaping power, you can step from or jump up onto a raised surface. Athletes who regularly train with plyometrics use wooden boxes that are padded and strong enough to support at least three times their weight. But you can also use a step or a sturdy bench as long as it is of sufficient height and width. An exercise mat or grass will provide cushioning for landing. For information about equipment, see the box on page 57.

To decide on the height of the box or other jumping surface, perform the jump-and-reach test. Stand beside a wall and, holding a piece of chalk, mark the highest point you can reach. Then jump as high as you can and reach up to mark the wall; the difference between the marks is your vertical jump height. You should be able to just reach your vertical jump height when performing the in-depth jump shown on page 80. Start with an eight-inch box. If you can reach your jump height, try a 12-inch box. If you can still reach your jump height, try a box of 18 inches. If you cannot reach your jump height, use the 12-inch box; if you reach your jump point, try a box six inches higher.

Be especially careful performing the in-depth jumps shown on pages 80-83. They are difficult as well as potentially injurious, and you should be in peak condition before you consider attempting them.

Stand relaxed, facing a box *(above)*. Bending at the hips and knees, use your arms as you jump up and forward onto the box *(center)*. Land on your feet with your waist, hips and knees flexed *(opposite)*.

# In-Depth Jump

Stand on top of the box (1), then step down onto a mat or grass (2), bending at the waist, hips and knees with your arms behind you as you land (3). Immediately jump up as high as you can, using your arms to help power yourself (4). Flex at your hips and knees as you land (5).

## Reverse In-Depth Jump

Stand on the box (1), then step backward with your right foot
(2). Flex your knees as you land and bring your arms behind you
(3). Jump up forcefully as fast as you can, using your arms (4).
Land with your knees and hips flexed (5).

# The Upper Body

Plyometric exercises for the upper body are usually performed with a medicine ball that weighs between three and 16 pounds. Throwing the medicine ball requires a total-body effort, and all your muscles must be strong if your throw is to be powerful and sufficient enough to carry the ball forward and upward.

For most of these exercises, you need to throw the ball by stepping forward first. Then you must transfer the force from your legs, through your body and into your arms. Some

exercises eliminate the need to step forward first, but the transfer of force from your torso to your arms is always necessary to complete the activity properly and effectively.

Select a medicine ball heavy enough that you must work hard during the exercise, but not so burdensome as to hamper your form.

You will find that the exercises require you to put your upper body through a greater range of motion than would be needed to perform similar throwing movements in various sports. This exaggerated range

of motion overloads your muscles just as increasing the weight of the medicine ball. The idea is similar to that of rapidly stretching the muscles to elicit the myotatic reflex (see page 56 for a description).

The exercises shown on pages 86-91 are best performed with a partner, but you can do them unassisted; the exercises on pages 84-85 and 92-95 require a partner. Choose someone with approximately the same strength and endurance as yourself so that you both get a good workout from the exercises.

**CHEST PASS** Stand about 10 feet away from your partner. Hold a medicine ball at chest level *(opposite)*. Step forward as you pass the ball to your partner, extending your arms at chest level *(center)*. As soon as you let go of the ball, turn your hands outward *(above)*.

# Overhead Pass

Hold a medicine ball at waist level *(inset above)*. Raise the ball back behind your head and flex your knees as you prepare to throw *(inset center)*. Step forward with your left leg and throw the ball by bringing it overhead *(inset right)*. Finish the throw by extending your arms and turning your palms downward *(right)*. Alternate legs when you repeat the exercise.

# Scoop Toss

Stand up straight while holding a medicine ball cupped in your hands. Flex your hips and knees until your thighs are parallel to the floor, bringing the ball between your legs (1). Raise the ball as you rise up and forward (2), extending your body as you toss the ball upward (3). Land with your arms at your sides and your knees flexed (4).

# Diagonal Pass

Stand with your knees flexed and your feet slightly apart, holding a medicine ball at chest level (1). Bring the ball back over your right shoulder as you lean backward (2). Step forward with your left leg as you throw the ball diagonally over your right shoulder. The ball should be in line with your right shoulder and your left hip (3). Your torso should be bent forward and turned slightly to the left with your palms outward (4). Alternate passes from both sides as you do the exercise.

# Medicine Ball Sit-Ups

Sit facing your partner with your knees and hips flexed and your legs interlocked. Hold a medicine ball overhead, leaning backward until you are nearly on the floor (1). Perform a sit-up, keeping your arms locked in the starting position, and release the ball when your torso is vertical (2). The force of the throw comes from your abdominals, not your arms. Your partner should catch the ball overhead, contracting his abdominals to prevent from falling backward (3). Then your partner performs a sit-up before throwing the ball (4).

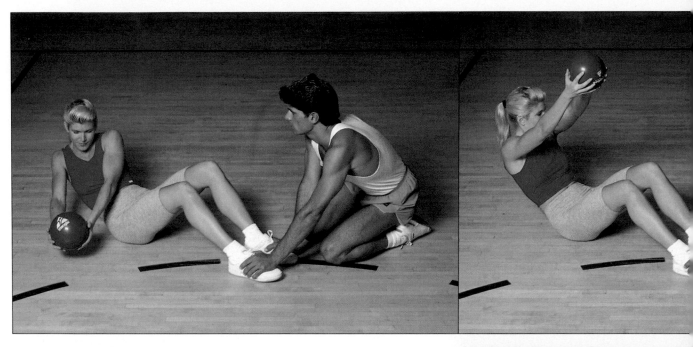

## Diagonal Twist

Hold a medicine ball cupped in your hands while sitting on the floor with your hips and knees flexed. Your partner secures your feet as you lean backward, forming a 90-degree angle at your waist. Twist your torso with your arms extended to the right a few inches above the floor (1). Raise the ball above your chest as you twist to your left (2). Continue to twist as you lower the ball to your left (3). Then twist to the right again, raising the ball (4), until you reach the starting position (5).

# CHAPTER FOUR

# Circuit Training

*A military-style workout for strengthening your muscles and cardiovascular system*

There is no master exercise that maintains all the various aspects of fitness. Running, for instance, is a great aerobic conditioner but does little to improve muscle strength. Chin-ups increase muscle power and endurance in your arms and shoulders, but contribute nothing to benefit your flexibility or aerobic capacity. Recognizing this problem, researchers at the University of Leeds in England developed circuit training — a method of conditioning that develops muscular strength and endurance, flexibility and aerobic fitness in a single program of exercises that are performed in a particular sequence.

The original circuits consisted of a series of six to 10 stations set up in a gymnasium or on a field. The circuit trainer would run between the stations, which were spaced apart at varying distances, and perform the exercises — for example, 25 sit-ups or 50 jumping jacks — at each stop. The longer the distance between stations, the greater the aerobic benefit the exerciser derived from performing the circuit.

Similarly, you could enhance the strength-building component by increasing the number of stations that involve muscle development.

Although slow to catch on at first, the idea of circuit training was marketed by several companies that developed circuit-training courses. These courses, laid out along running trails, resemble military obstacle courses, with nine to 18 stations that contain simple apparatus for performing a variety of warm-ups, and such exercises as jumping jacks, chin-ups, sit-ups, push-ups and balancing routines. Many circuits include not only aerobic and strength-building exercises, but also routines for coordination and stretching that provide a workout that encompasses all the elements of fitness. One manufacturer has installed more than 3,500 circuit courses in public parks, schools, hotels, office parks and military bases. In one survey of corporate employees who used a circuit-training course, many of them reported that they lost weight, felt better, slept more soundly and had more energy as a result.

Since you must do something different at every station, the tedium of an extended bout of repeated exercise is relieved by circuit training. In a well-designed circuit, you start slowly to ensure an adequate warm-up, and you perform exercises of gradually increasing difficulty. The stations are arranged to provide a specific sequence of exercise for the upper body, the abdominals and the legs. Finally, the intensity of the workout is gradually reduced to cool you down safely.

You do not need a formal or permanent course of stations to derive the benefits of circuit training. The regimen presented in this chapter involves a minimum amount of equipment, yet it provides a physically challenging series of stations for a full-body workout tailored to your own needs and pace. The exercises are based on training routines used at the United States Military Academy at West Point, and many of them are arranged in mini-circuits, in which each station consists of a multiple set of exercises designed to enhance a specific component of fitness — for example, muscular endurance — and condition a particular part of your body.

It is not necessary or even desirable to perform all of these circuits every day; rather, a workout should consist of three or four of them. You can also incorporate one or more of the mini-circuits at the conclusion of an aerobic workout, such as a long run or a stationary bicycle session. In each circuit, you should perform every exercise that is included. Then, for your next workout, choose a different combination of circuits. When you choose a set of circuits, pick a combination of both moderate and difficult exercises that condition both your upper and lower body. This allows you to derive the greatest benefit without becoming exhausted. Also, alternate upper and lower body exercises within each workout. *(For a guide to circuit combinations, see the box on the next page.)*

You can perform many of these circuits indoors by jogging in place or alternating jumping jacks between stations, or you can circuit train in your backyard or around your neighborhood. If you live near a

# Circuit Combinations

*It is not necessary to incorporate every circuit shown in this chapter in every training session. For variety — as well as to give yourself a rest — you can omit or substitute some circuits for others on alternate days. No matter what combination you use, however, you should always include a five- to 10-minute warm-up and stretching session at the beginning of each workout, and a five-minute cool-down at the end. In addition, you should also perform the abdominal crunches and lifts (pages 104-109), or a few of the exercises, at least three or four times per week. The following is a sample weekly schedule that employs a hard day/easy day concept, which means you alternate days of strenuous exercise with ones that are relatively easy.*

◆ **MONDAY:** Warm-ups and Stretches *(pages 100-103)*, 20-minute run, Two-for-One Calisthenics *(pages 122-127)*, Horizontal Ladder Circuit *(pages 118-121)*, Lifts and Crunches *(pages 104-109)*, cool-down.

◆ **TUESDAY:** Warm-ups and Stretches *(pages 100-103)*, Leg Workers Circuit *(pages 114-117)*, Push-Up Circuit *(pages 132-137)*, Lifts and Crunches *(pages 104-109)*, cool-down.

◆ **WEDNESDAY:** Warm-ups and Stretches *(pages 100-103)*, Hill Running *(pages 112-113)*, Sandbag Circuit *(pages 128-131)*, cool-down.

◆ **THURSDAY:** Warm-ups and Stretches *(pages 100-103)*, Rope Climbing *(pages 138-141)*, 20- to 30-minute run or Leg Workers Circuit *(pages 114-117)*, Two-for-One Calisthenics *(pages 122-127)*, twistie and straight crunches *(pages 106-107)*, cool-down.

◆ **FRIDAY:** Warm-ups and Stretches *(pages 100-103)*, Stair Circuit *(pages 110-111)*, Push-Up Circuit *(pages 132-137)*, Lifts and Crunches *(pages 104-109)*, cool-down.

◆ **SATURDAY:** Warm-ups and Stretches *(pages 100-103)*, 30-minute jog, Horizontal Ladder Circuit *(pages 118-121)*, Lifts and Crunches *(pages 104-109)*.

◆ **SUNDAY:** Rest

school with a playground, for instance, you can make use of the horizontal ladder as a station to perform pull-ups and other exercises *(see pages 118-121)*. If the school has a football field or track, you can run up the bleachers or stadium stairs as a station for building leg endurance *(see pages 110-111)*.

Many of the exercises that follow are quite strenuous. In order to work out at a level intense enough to achieve fitness benefits, yet not so strenuous that you become injured, you must listen to your body and monitor how you feel. If you find that performing a particular mini-circuit leaves you feeling exhausted and sore, you can cut back to a more manageable level. In addition, if there are any exercises in this chapter that are difficult for you to perform safely, such as the supine leg lifts on page 106 or the rope climb on pages 138-141, skip them entirely or perform them at a lower intensity until you have attained sufficient strength and agility.

# Warm-Ups and Stretches

The warm-up exercises and stretches shown on these two pages and the following two are specific movements designed to prepare your body for the more vigorous activities that follow. Some of the later routines are extremely strenuous and require a maximum range of motion in your joints and muscles. In order to avoid injury and derive the greatest benefit from circuit training, it is essential that you warm up thoroughly.

Once your body begins warming up, oxygen exchange between the blood and the muscles is enhanced, metabolic chemical reactions take place at a faster rate and nervous impulses fire more quickly. Moreover, warming up decreases the internal friction of your muscles and joints.

Stretching after you have warmed up increases muscle flexibility and helps minimize the risk of musculoskeletal injury. Most experts agree that tight, inflexible muscles are prone to pulls, tears and other stresses and injuries.

Begin your warm-up session with one minute of marching in place, then follow with the exercises shown at right. When you have finished them, run in place for another 60 seconds before progressing to the following pages. Once you have completed the stretches shown on pages 102-103, repeat all of them again for your opposite limbs.

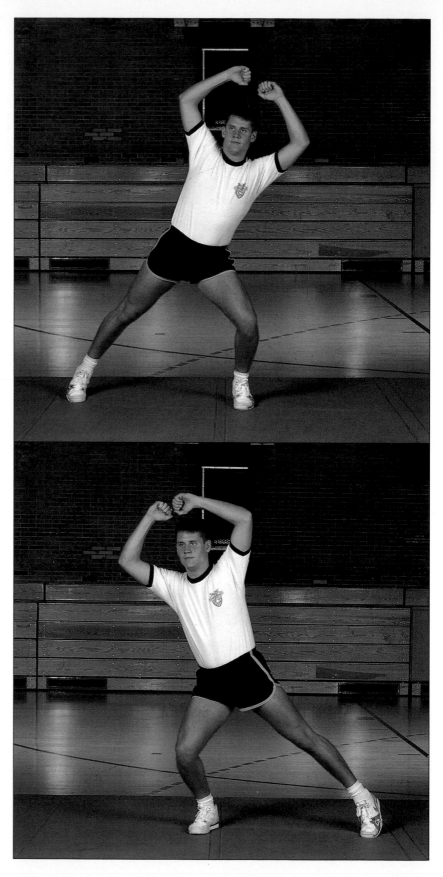

**LOW-IMPACT JACKS** Stand with your hands at your sides, your knees flexed slightly and your back straight. Raise your hands over your head and swing your right leg to the side *(above)*. Return to the starting position. Raise your hands again and swing your left leg to the side *(right)*. Repeat the exercise for 60 seconds.

**ALTERNATE KNEE LIFTS** Stand erect with your knees bent slightly and interlace your fingers behind your head. Twist your torso to the right and lift your right knee toward your left elbow *(above left)*. Return to the starting position, then twist your torso to the left and lift your left knee toward your right elbow *(above)*. Return to the starting position. Continue for 60 seconds.

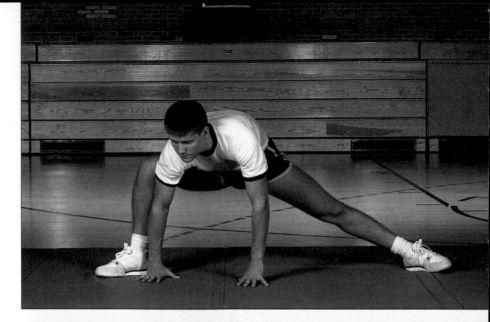

**SPIDER** Bend over and position your hands on the floor with your elbows inside your knees, which you should not bend more than 90 degrees. Extend your left leg to the side *(right)*. Hold for at least 10-15 seconds.

**LUNGE** From the spider position, keep your feet in place and swing your body to the right, moving your hands to both sides of your right foot *(right)*. Try to drop your hips to the floor, keeping your back leg straight. Hold for 10-15 seconds.

**QUAD STRETCH** From the lunge position, drop your left knee to the floor and grasp your left heel with your right hand. Draw your heel toward your buttocks *(right)*. Hold for 10-15 seconds.

**HAMSTRING STRETCH** Return your right hand next to your right foot, extend your left leg and place your foot flat on the floor. Raise your right toes *(left)*. Hold the stretch for 10-15 seconds.

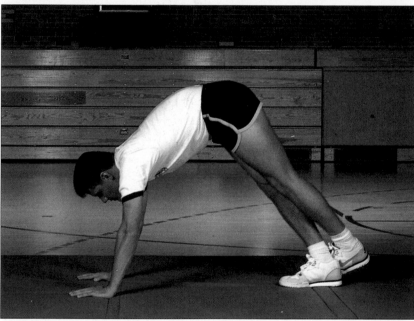

**CALF STRETCH** Draw your right leg back next to your left leg and place your palms flat on the floor. Swing your left foot behind your right heel and press it against the floor *(left)*. Hold for 10-15 seconds.

**LOW BACK STRETCH** Sit on the floor, draw your knees to your chest and grasp your toes *(left)*. Hold for 10-15 seconds. Start over again and repeat all the stretches using your opposite limbs.

# Lifts and Crunches

**M**any people neglect their abdominal muscles when they work out. However, strong abdominals are important for good posture, and they eliminate strain on the lower back. Along with well-toned abdominals, strong hip flexor muscles, which you use to lift your knees, help reduce the risk of lower back injuries.

The exercises on pages 104-109 will develop muscular strength and conditioning in the abdominals and hip flexors. They should be performed three or four times a week, as outlined in the box on page 99. If any exercise causes back pain, stop immediately and cut back on the number of repetitions in future workouts until you build up more abdominal strength. Perform them in the order presented so that the upper-abdominal stabilizing fibers do not become fatigued.

**LEG LIFTS** Hang from a bar with your hands shoulder-width apart. Lift your knees toward your chest, keeping your lower back rounded so that your pelvis is rotated forward *(inset).* Begin with 15 bent-knee lifts. Rest 10 seconds and repeat. As you get stronger, straighten your legs to increase the effort *(right).* When you can, perform 10 straight-leg lifts, then five with bent knees. Rest for 10-15 seconds and repeat.

## LIFTS AND CRUNCHES
*(continued)*

**SUPINE LEG LIFTS** Lie on an exercise mat with your hands under your pelvis to prevent arching. Lift your head and raise your legs 12 inches off the floor *(right)*. Rock your pelvis and raise your legs 18 inches off the floor *(far right)*. Alternate between 12 and 18 inches for 25 reps. Rest for 10 seconds; repeat 20 times.

**TWISTIE CRUNCHES** Lie on your back with your hands behind your head, knees bent and feet flat on the floor. Lift your head and turn your torso to the right *(right)*. Leading with your left elbow, rise into a crunch and hold for a full second *(far right)*. Maintain the twist throughout the range of motion. Perform 20 reps for the left side, then repeat for the right side without resting.

**STRAIGHT CRUNCHES** Remain on your back with your hands behind your head and your feet flat on the floor *(right)*. Slowly raise your shoulders off the ground no more than six to eight inches *(far right)*. Hold for one second and return to the starting position. Perform 30 reps.

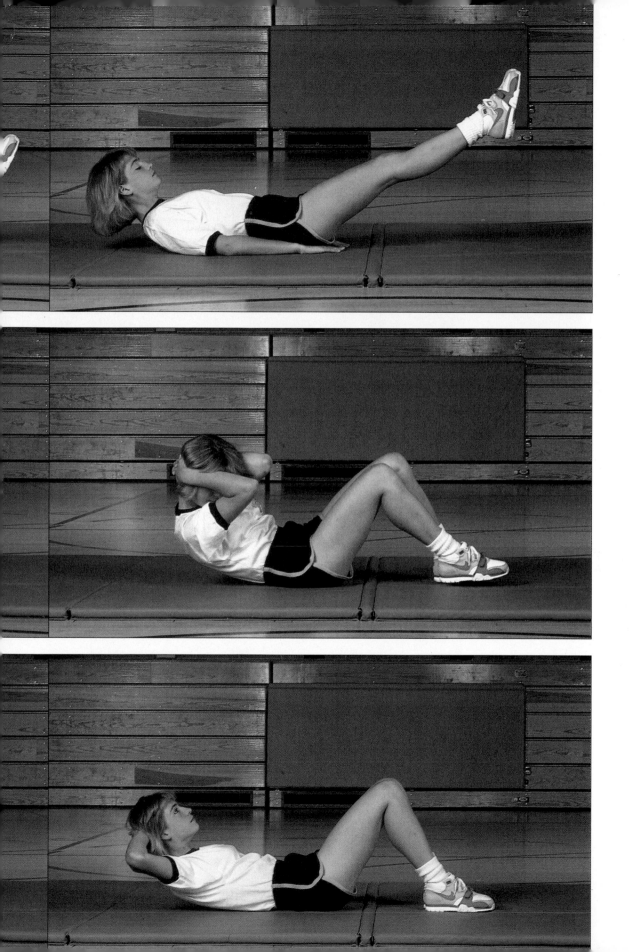

## LIFTS AND CRUNCHES
*(continued)*

**BICYCLE** Keep your hands behind your head, extend your legs and sit up. Draw your right knee up and twist your body to the right, bringing your left elbow toward your knee *(right)*. Then extend your right leg, draw your left knee up and twist your right elbow toward the knee *(far right)*. Perform 30 repetitions.

**ROCKER** Lie on your back with your feet flat on the floor. Place your arms at your sides with your palms down *(right)*. Rock onto your upper back and draw your knees to your chest *(far right)*. Hold for a second, then return to the starting position. Repeat 15-20 times at a moderate pace.

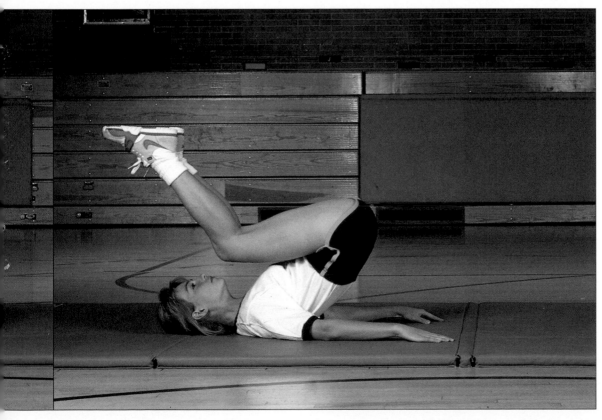

# Stair Circuit

According to one exercise physiologist, running up stairs is seldom incorporated in a training routine. Because most steps are the same height and most staircases rise at the same angle, they all provide about the same level of challenge. Running up stairs is a powerful exercise for the legs and helps develop both muscular endurance and cardiovascular fitness.

Find a staircase that has a landing after 18 to 24 steps, like those found in many stadiums or schools. Do not try to run up a larger number of steps at one time, since this will provide you with too much recovery time as you jog down the stairs. Make sure you are warmed up sufficiently before you begin, then proceed with the stair-running exercises at right. The complete circuit consists of 10 repetitions of stair running, then two reps of stair hopping on each leg, ten more runs, and finally, jumping up the stairs for two reps; this should take 20 minutes to complete. If you feel unsteady or dizzy at any point during the one-leg hops, stop immediately and do not continue.

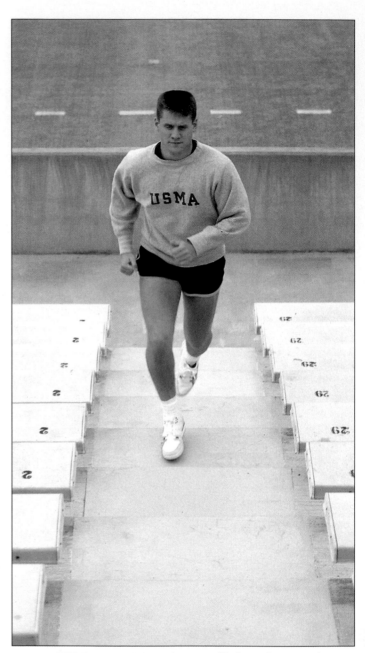

**RUN** Run up and down the steps 10 times. Do not push yourself too hard; but at the same time, do not rest between each repetition; pace yourself carefully so that you do not become exhausted.

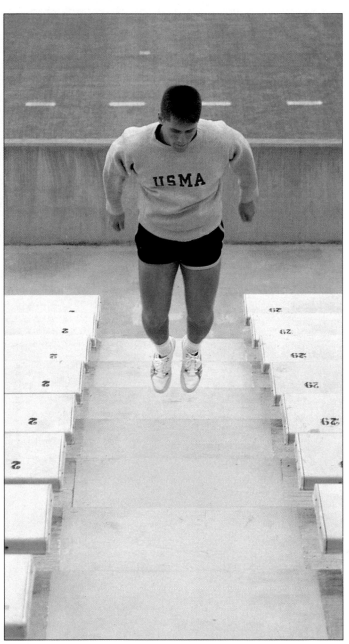

**ONE-LEG HOP** Hop up the stairs on your left leg and jog down on both legs; repeat. Hop up on your right leg and jog down on both legs; repeat. Then run up and down 10 times on both legs.

**TWO-LEG JUMP** After you have repeated running up and down the stairs 10 times on both legs, jump up the stairs with both feet together. Jog down and repeat jumping up on two feet.

# Hill Running

Hills will give you about the same training benefits that running up and down stairs does, except that every hill is different, providing a specific level of challenge. To ensure a good workout, find a hill that has a 10- to 12-percent incline and measure off a distance up the hill of approximately 300 yards.

To perform your hill workout, sprint up the 300 yards and then walk or jog back down. Repeat this six to eight times, and then add reps until you can perform it 10 to 12 times. In a beginning program, you may run up the hill in one minute and 30 to 45 seconds, and jog or walk down it in about two minutes. As you gain strength and speed, it may take you only 1:15 to 1:30 to run up a hill.

When you run up a hill, lean forward slightly to give yourself momentum and the sensation that you are "falling" up the hill. Pump your arms powerfully and imagine that you are using them to pull yourself up on a rope. Look at a point on the road about 30 feet in front of you rather than looking at your feet or the crest of the hill.

1

2

# Leg Workers Circuit

This circuit of exercises will help develop muscular endurance in the most powerful muscles of your body, namely the quadriceps and hamstrings, the gluteals in your buttocks and the gastrocnemius muscles in your calves. The complete circuit consists of the bench steps, sissy squats and heel raises performed continuously as shown without rest; you can do one or more sets of this circuit.

For the bench step and heel raise exercises, men should find a bench that is 15 to 18 inches high; most women will be more comfortable with a 13- to 15-inch bench. Make sure the bench is sturdy and will not tip when you use it. Benches in stadiums or gymnasiums are often ideal for this purpose.

Be sure that you maintain good posture throughout the circuit and do not strain your back by leaning over or arching. Again, these exercises can be strenuous. Stop immediately if you become exhausted or are in danger of losing your balance.

**3** **4**

**BENCH STEPS** Stand in front of the bench and step up with your right foot (1). Then step up with your left (2). Step down with your left (3), and then with your right (4). In this exercise, one step is complete after both feet are on the ground in the starting position. Perform at a pace of 40-45 steps per minute for five minutes. Change your lead leg after every five to eight steps.

## LEG WORKERS *(continued)*

**SISSY SQUATS** This exercise is quite strenuous despite its name. Stand next to a railing or some other stationary object and extend both arms to your sides, holding the railing with one hand for stability. Bend your knees and drop your pelvis over your heels (1). Straighten your knees and repeat five to eight times. Then bend your knees, drop your pelvis and move it forward until it is over your toes (2). Keeping your back straight, rock back and forth, shifting the location of your pelvis from over your toes to over your heels five to eight times. Return to a standing position, then bend your knees, move your pelvis until it is over your toes, and straighten your legs while rising on the balls of your feet (3). Continue straightening your legs (4), and return to a standing position (5). Repeat five to eight times.

**HEEL RAISES** Stand on the balls of your feet at the edge of a bench or stadium seat. Hold onto a railing or some other stationary object. Lift your heels *(right)*, and then lower them 20 times. Then drop your heels below the level of the seat *(far right)*, and hold this calf muscle stretch for 30 seconds. Repeat the sequence twice.

**RUNG SERIES** Warm up with 100 jumping jacks, then jump up to hang from the first rung of a horizontal ladder. Perform two pull-ups *(right)*. Move forward three rungs *(center right)*, then perform two more pull-ups. Continue in this manner until you reach the end of the ladder. Perform two final pull-ups, and then three to five bent-knee leg lifts *(far right)*.

# Horizontal Ladder Circuit

In order to perform this series of exercises, you must have access to a playground area or a gym with a horizontal ladder setup. Although children love to use horizontal ladders for play, this equipment can be a powerful conditioner for grip strength and the muscles of your forearms, upper arms, the hip flexor muscles and the latissimus dorsi in your back. In addition, you will be deriving some cardiovascular benefit from the jumping jacks in this mini-circuit. To perform this circuit correctly, you must be able to do pull-ups. If you have difficulty, a partner can help lift you.

You can traverse the horizontal ladder in two ways — either by gripping each horizontal rung one after the other in the traditional method or by gripping the side piece and moving hand over hand. The sequence shown on this and the facing page shows the horizontal-rung series, while pages 120 and 121 show the sidepiece series.

When you perform this circuit, alternate the rung and sidepiece series twice. Perform eight to 10 pull-ups on one pass across the bars, unless the number of horizontal rungs limits you to six pull-ups on each pass. In that case, increase the number of pull-ups you perform at the beginning or the end of each pass.

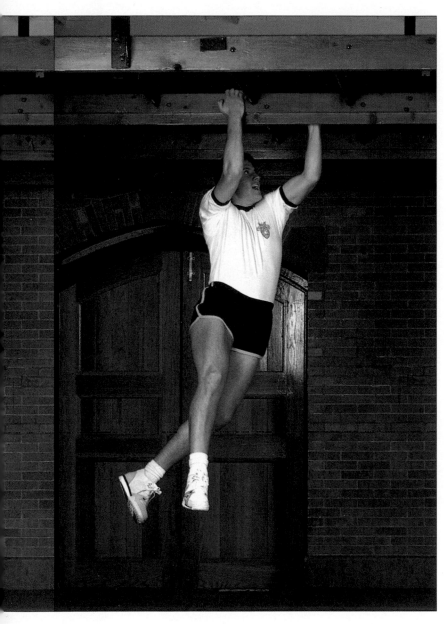

**SIDEPIECE SERIES** Jump up and hold onto one of the parallel bars with both hands and perform three to five pull-ups so that you bring your left ear to the sidepiece *(far left).* Then do three to five pull-ups to your right ear *(center left).* Traverse the sidepiece hand over hand (left). At the end of the support, do three to five more left- and right-ear pull-ups.

# Two-for-One Calisthenics

Most of the exercise sets in this circuit condition two body parts at once, hence the two-for-one name. The title has a double meaning, since you also will be performing these activities at a certain beat that involves a slow count and half counts. These particular exercises are best performed at a tempo of 120 beats per minute; you can listen to music. Count the beats — two per second — to yourself.

Pace yourself as follows: When you do the push-ups, start in the up position and lower yourself, allowing two counts. Then go up for two counts. Now double your time so that you lower on the next count — five — and push up on six. Then come down on seven and push up on eight. On the count of eight, you should have completed three push-ups, one of them slowly and the other two quickly. Perform three more sequences of eight counts each — for nine more push-ups and a total of 32 counts — and then progress to the next activity.

Do all the exercises on these two pages, and then repeat the push-ups to finish the circuit. Four 32-count exercises comprise one set. Perform one or two more sets as you become stronger. As an alternate Two-for-One series, you can perform the movements on pages 124-127. As an advanced Two-for-One, you can combine the exercises on these two pages with those that follow. The alternates are particularly strenuous; do not attempt them unless your abdominals are strong.

**MOUNTAIN CLIMBER** Place your hands on the floor shoulder-width apart and extend your legs behind you. Without touching your right foot on the floor, draw your right knee to your chest *(far left)*. Return your right leg to the extended position and then raise your left knee *(left)*.

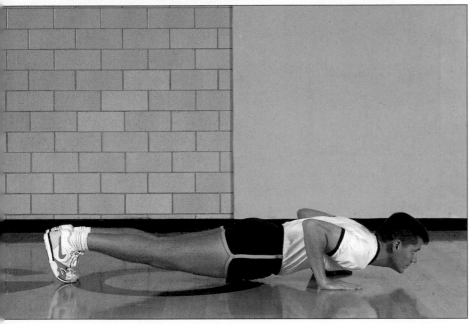

**PUSH-UPS** From the mountain climber, keep your arms straight and flatten your palms on the floor. Extend both legs and keep your back straight *(far left)*. Bend your elbows and lower your chest to an inch or two off the floor *(left)*.

**BOTTOMS UP** From the extended push-up position, thrust forward with your toes and lift your buttocks up so that the bottom of your spine points toward the ceiling *(far left)*. Jump back with your toes to the starting position *(left)*. Avoid arching your back. Repeat the push-ups.

123

# Two-for-One Alternates

**CRAB PUSH-UPS** Sit on the floor and raise yourself up on your feet and hands, with fingers pointing to your heels. Lift your chest and pelvis up and keep your elbows extended *(right)*. Drop your body toward the floor by bending your elbows *(far right)*.

**BICYCLE** Sit on the floor with your legs extended and your fingers intertwined behind your head. Bring your left knee up and swing your right elbow to meet it *(right)*. Extend your left knee and draw up your right knee, meeting it with your left elbow *(far right)*. Do not arch your back.

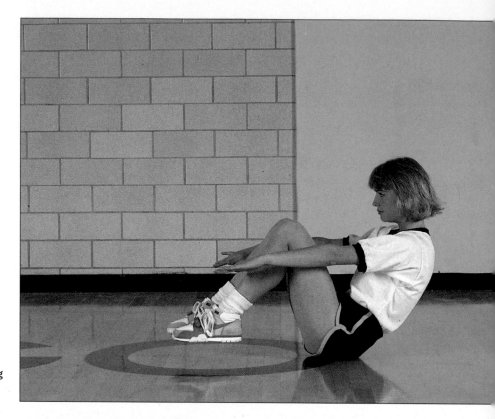

**ROW** Sit with both knees drawn up, feet off the floor and your arms extended parallel to the floor in front of you *(right)*. Pull your arms back as if you were rowing a boat, and extend your legs *(far right)*. Do not arch your back.

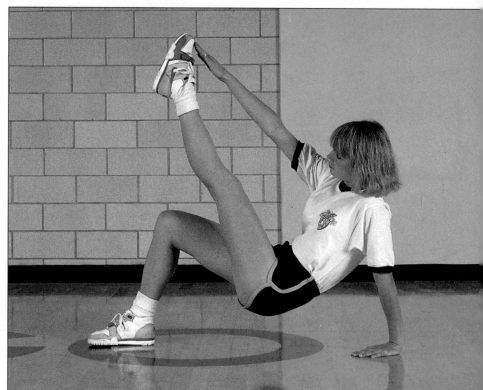

**DIAGONAL TOE TOUCH** Supported by your hands and feet, lift your pelvis off the floor. Extend your left foot toward the ceiling and touch your toes with your right hand *(right)*. Return your foot and hand to the floor, then extend your right foot toward the ceiling and touch your toes with your left hand *(far right)*.

# Sandbag Circuit

This circuit contains a number of resistance-training exercises similar to lifting weights. To perform this series, you need some burlap bags filled with sand. Using sandbags is convenient and makes it easy to adjust the weight as you increase your strength. You can fill bags and weigh them on scales. Men may fill two bags each for 25, 30 and 40 or 50 pounds. Women may fill two bags each for 15, 20 and 25 pounds. Experiment to find the most appropriate resistance for each exercise.

In addition to the exercises shown here, you can add several more. Perform crunches, on pages 106-107, with a sandbag on your chest. You can also do side lateral raises by holding sandbags at your sides and raising them until your arms are parallel to the floor, or biceps curls, bending your elbows.

Perform each exercise continuously for one minute. Then run double time in place for one minute before moving on to the next exercise. Finish with a double-time run and start the circuit over again.

**LUNGE** Attach a rope to two heavy sandbags and wrap a towel around the rope so that you can drape it comfortably over your shoulders. Stand erect and hold the sandbags to keep them steady *(above left)*. Take one step forward with your right foot and drop down so that your left knee comes within an inch of the floor *(above)*. Return to the starting position by pushing off the right foot. Repeat on your left leg.

**BENT-OVER ROW** Hold two moderate to heavy sandbags at your sides, keep your knees bent slightly, and bend over so that the sandbags are several inches off the floor *(above left)*. Lift the sandbags until your hands are at hip level *(above)*. Return to the starting position.

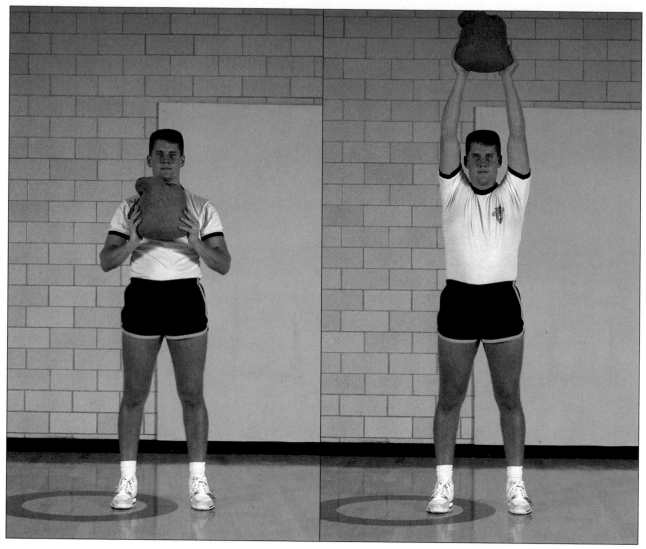

**MILITARY PRESS** Stand with your feet apart and your knees bent slightly, holding a sandbag in front of you at chest level *(above left)*. Lift the sandbag directly over your head *(above)*. Avoid arching your back. Return to the starting position.

**TRICEPS LIFT** Stand erect and hold a sandbag with both hands over and behind your head so that the sandbag hangs behind your back *(above left)*. Extend your arms and lift the sandbag directly up *(above)*. Avoid arching your back. Return to the starting position.

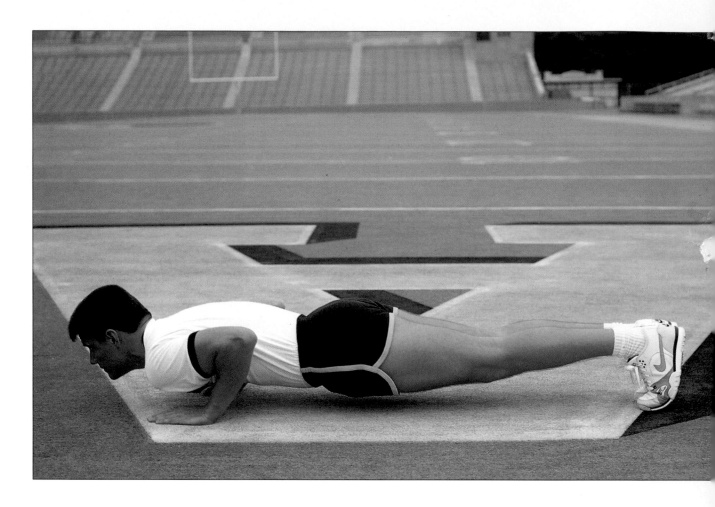

# Push-Up Circuit

The push-up is an effective upper body conditioner, particularly for building upper arm, shoulder and chest muscle strength and endurance. Push-ups also help develop strength in your abdominal muscles and lower back, since these areas help to stabilize you while you perform this exercise.

In addition to the classic push-up, for which you place your hands on the ground directly under your shoulders, there are a number of variations that help target particular muscles. The push-up on this and the facing page demonstrates proper posture in both the up and down positions for the three push-up variations shown on pages 133-134. The push-up circuit continues on pages 136-137, but with different postures, including piked and crab variations.

You can add this upper body mini-circuit to almost any workout. Unless otherwise directed, perform each type of push-up repeatedly for 30 seconds without rest before progressing to the next push-up.

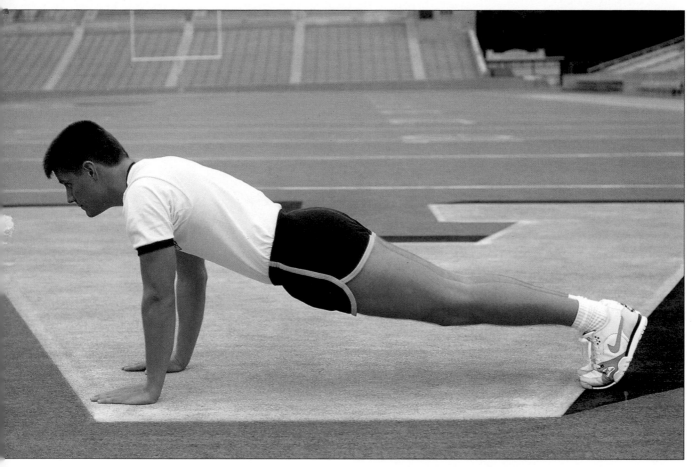

In the down push-up position, keep your hands flat on the ground, your chest an inch or two above it, and your body and head aligned *(opposite)*. As you push up, extend your arms but do not lock your elbows, keeping your back straight *(above)*.

## PUSH-UP CIRCUIT *(continued)*

Perform the diamond push-up by placing your hands on the ground so that your thumbs and forefingers form a diamond *(above left)*. Next, do a narrow-grip push-up with your hands placed under your shoulders *(above)*. Then perform a wide-grip push-up with your hands wider than your shoulders *(right)*.

**PIKED PUSH-UPS** Bend at the hip and make your body into a bridge *(top)*. Making sure to keep your body bent at the same angle, slowly lower yourself until your nose comes within an inch or two of the ground *(above)*.

**CRAB PUSH-UPS** With your feet and hands flat, lift your pelvis up until you are parallel to the ground *(top)*. By bending your arms, lower yourself to within a few inches of the ground *(above)*. Do as many as you can in 15 seconds.

**THE CLINCH** Grip the rope with both hands at about face level and raise your right foot up so that the rope rests against the inside of your knee and the outside of your foot *(above left)*. Holding yourself in place with your hands, lift your left leg up and cross your feet to squeeze the rope between your thighs, just above your knees, and the outside edges of your shoes. Hang on the rope in a sitting position *(above right)*.

# Rope Climbing

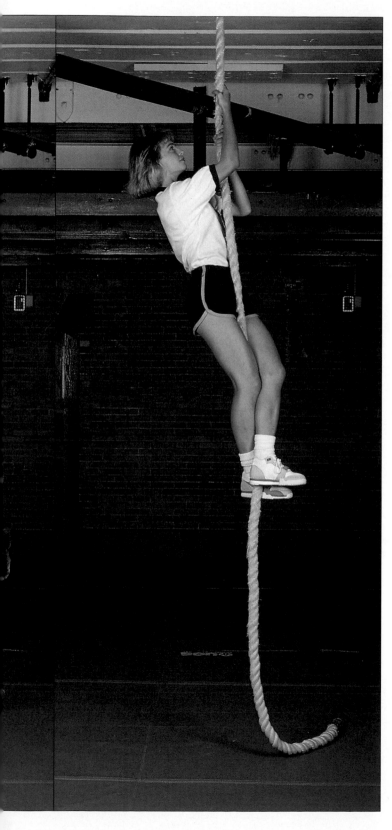

Because it is sometimes essential in combat situations or during troop maneuvers, rope climbing has long been a staple of military training. And, although it is not often included in nonmilitary fitness programs, climbing is a superb whole-body muscle strengthener — an effective conditioner for anyone. Not only does it strengthen your upper arms and hand grip, but it conditions your abdominal muscles and thighs as well. Most hemp ropes are too thin and rough for comfortable climbing, but many high school and college gyms have rope apparatus made for climbing.

Safety on the ropes is crucial. Always set up mats under the rope. If you are a climbing novice, make sure you have a spotter, and do not climb more than six feet off the ground. Begin by climbing slowly until you have mastered the technique, then perform repeat rope climbs until you have climbed a total of 40 to 60 feet.

**ASCENDING** Keep the rope squeezed between your thighs and shoes. Extend your legs forward so you feel like you are stepping on the rope. Walk your hands up the rope as you extend your legs *(far left)*. To continue, hold the rope tightly with your hands but relax the grip of your thighs and feet. Slide your thighs and feet up until you reach the sitting position again, then clinch. Walk up the rope with your hands and extend your legs until your body is straight *(left)*.

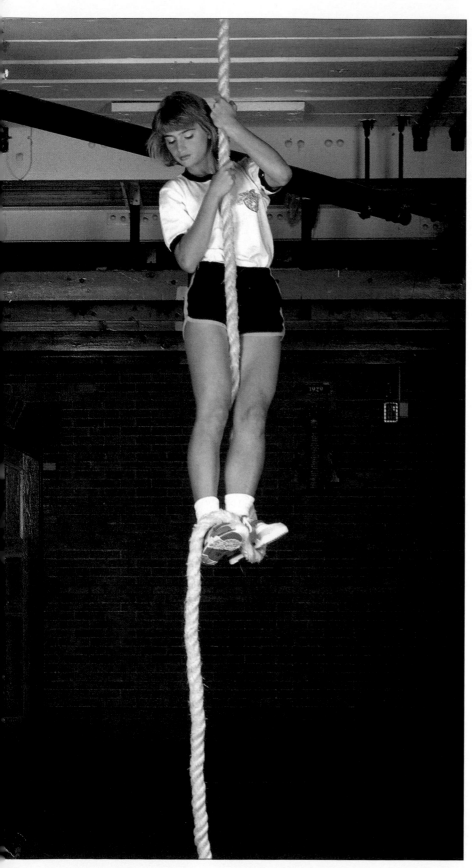

## ROPE CLIMBING
*(continued)*

**DESCENDING** Once you have reached the top of your climb, lock your feet. From the clinch, drag your left heel across the top of your right foot, with the rope squeezed between them *(far left)*. The rope will loop between your feet so that if you squeeze your feet together, you will be firmly locked in place. Release just enough tension between your feet so you can slide down the rope under control by walking down hand under hand *(left)*.

## PROP CREDITS

Cover: tank top and shorts–Athletic Style, New York City, body balls–SLM Action Sports, Inc., Morrisville, N.C.; page 6: shorts–Athletic Style, New York City; page 18: tank top–Dance France, LTD, Santa Monica, Calif., tights–Athletic Style, New York City; pages 22-53: chairs–Conran's, New York City, area rug–ABC International Design Rugs, New York City, white towels–Martex, New York City, leotard and tights–Dance France, LTD, Santa Monica, Calif., tank top–The Finals, Port Jervis, N.Y., shorts and shoes–Athletic Style, New York City; page 54: shoes–Nautilus Athletic Footwear, Inc., Greenville, S.C.; page 58-69: tank tops and shorts–Athletic Style, New York City, shoes–Nautilus Athletic Footwear, Inc., Greenville, S.C.; pages 70-77: tank top–Hind Performance, San Luis Obispo, Calif., shorts–Athletic Style, New York City, shoes–Nautilus Athletic Footwear, Inc., Greenville, S.C.; pages 78-85: tank top and shorts–Athletic Style, New York City, shoes–Nautilus Athletic Footwear, Inc., Greenville, S.C.; pages 84-95: tank top–Hind Performance, San Luis Obispo, Calif., shorts–Athletic Style, New York City, shoes–Nautilus Athletic Footwear, Inc., Greenville, S.C., body balls, SLM Action Sports, Inc., Morrisville, N.C.; pages 92-95: tank top and shorts–Athletic Style, New York City, shoes–Nautilus Athletic Footwear, Inc., Greenville, S.C.; page 96: tights–The Finals, Port Jervis, N.Y.; pages 100-141: location courtesy of the United States Military Academy, West Point, NY, air trainers–Nike, Inc., Beaverton, Ore.

## ACKNOWLEDGMENTS

All cosmetics and grooming products supplied by Clinique Labs, Inc., New York City

Nutrition analysis provided by Hill Nutrition Associates, Fayetteville, N.Y.

Off-camera warm-up equipment: rowing machine supplied by Precor USA, Redmond, Wash.; Tunturi stationary bicycle supplied by Amerec Corp., Bellevue, Wash.

Washing machine and dryer supplied by White-Westinghouse, Columbus, Ohio

Index prepared by Ian Tucker

Production by Giga Communications

## PHOTOGRAPHY CREDITS

Exercise photgraphs by Andrew Eccles.

## ILLUSTRATION CREDITS

Pages 9, 10, 13, illustrations: David Flaherty.

*Time-Life Books, Inc. offers a wide range of fine recordings, including a* Rock 'n' Roll Era *series. For subscription information, call 1-800-621-7026, or write TIME-LIFE MUSIC, P. O. Box C-32068; Richmond, Virginia 23261-2068.*

# INDEX

Abdominal exercises
  calisthenics, 29-37
  circuit training, 104, 106-109, 124-125
abdominal strength assessment, 13
amino acid assessment, 15
arm strength assessment, 13

Bench steps, 115
bent-over rowing, 129
bicycle exercise, 108-109, 124-125
bottoms up, 123
bounding, 77
box routines, 78-83
breathing, 20-21
broad jump, standing, 68-69

Calf stretches, 103
calisthenics, 19-53
  alternation of exercises, 20
  breathing, 20
  control of resistance in, 9, 10
  demi-squats, 51
  diagonal thigh lifts, 43
  double leg extensions, 30-31
  double leg lifts, 29
  double leg raises, 32-33
  full squats, 52-53
  hamstring-gluteus bends, 48
  hamstring lifts, 43
  hip balances, 43
  hip drops, 26
  hip rotations, 24-25
  inner thigh lifts, 41
  lower body exercises, 38-53
  middle body exercises, 29-37
  muscle co-contraction and, 8
  negative sit-ups, 34-35
  outer thigh lifts, 45-47
  push-ups, 22-23, 123, 124
  repetitions, 20
  scapular shrugs, 27
  total body crunches, 36-37
  triangle lifts, 39
  triangle presses, 39
  two-for-one, 122-127
  upper body exercises, 22-27
  variety in, 19-20
  warm-ups, 21
  workout progressions, 21
carbohydrates, 14
chest passes, 85
circuit training, 97-141
  combinations, 98, 99
  crunches, 104, 106-109
  defined, 10

  early, 97-98
  hill running, 112-113
  horizontal ladder, 118-121
  leg lifts, 104-107
  leg workers, 114-117
  push-ups, 123-125, 132-137
  rope climbing, 138-141
  sandbag, 128-131
  stairs, 110-111
  stretches, 100-103
  two-for-one calisthenics, 122-127
  warm-ups, 100-103
clinches, 138
cone hops, 70-71
  lateral, 72-73
cool-downs, 12
  for calisthenics, 21
  for plyometrics, 57
crab push-ups, 124-125, 137
crunches, 104, 106-109
  bicycle, 108-109
  rocker, 108-109
  straight, 106-107
  total body, 36-37
  twistie, 106-107

Demi-squats, 51
detraining, 11
diagonal passes, 90-91
diagonal thigh lifts, 43
diagonal toe touches, 126-127
diagonal twists, 94-95
diamond push-ups, 134
double leg extensions, 30-31
double leg lifts, 29
double leg raises, 32-33
double-leg tuck jumps, 62-63

Endurance, see muscular endurance
exercise mat, 57
exercise programs
  calisthenics, see calisthenics
  circuit training, see circuit training
  detraining, 11
  muscle firmness and shape, elements of, 8
  myth of power eating, 14-17
  physique and, 8
  plateaus, 11
  plyometrics, see plyometrics
  self-assessment, 12-13
  strength training and muscle power, 10
  workout frequency, 12
explosive power, 10

Fat, dietary, 14

Gluteus-hamstring bends, 48

Hamstring
  -gluteus bends, 48
  lifts, 49
  stretches, 103
heel raises, 117
hill running, 112-113
hip
  balances, 43
  drops, 26
  kickers, 59
  rotations, 24-25
horizontal ladder circuit, 118-121

In-depth jumps, 80-81
  reverse, 82-83
inner thigh lifts, 41

Jacks, low-impact, 100
jumping surfaces, 57

Knee
  lifts, alternate, 101
  push-ups, 23

Lateral cone hops, 72-73
leg extensions, double, 29
leg lifts, 104-107
  double, 29
  supine, 106-107
leg raises, double, 32-33
leg workers circuit, 114-117
lifts
  leg, see leg lifts
  triceps, 131
low back stretches, 103
lower body exercises
  calisthenics, 38-53
  plyometrics, 58-83
low-impact jacks, 100
lunges, 102
  with sandbags, 128

Medicine ball exercises
  diagonal twists, 94-95
  passes, 84-91
  sit-ups, 92-93
  medicine balls, 57
middle body exercises, calisthenics, 29-37
military presses, 130
mountain climber exercise, 123
muscle co-contraction, 8
muscle contractions, 8, 11, 56
muscle power, 10, 55-56

muscle strength
 assessment of, 12-13
 defined, 8
 muscle power and, 10, 55-56
muscular endurance
 calisthenics and, 19, 20
 defined, 8
myotatic reflex, 56

**N**arrow-grip push-ups, 134
negative sit-ups, 34-35

**O**ne-leg hops, 111
outer thigh lifts, 45-47
overhead passes, 86-87

**P**asses, medicine ball, 84-91
physique, 8
piked push-ups, 136
plyometrics, 55-95
 basis for, 55-56
 bounding, 77
 box routines, 78-83
 chest passes, 85
 cone hops, 70-71
 defined, 10-11
 diagonal passes, 90-91
 diagonal twists, 94-95
 double-leg tuck jumps, 62-63
 equipment for, 57
 hip kickers, 59
 in-depth jumps, 80-81
 lateral cone hops, 72-73
 lower body exercises, 58-83
 medicine ball sit-ups, 92-93
 overhead passes, 86-87
 phases in, 56
 power skipping, 75
 reverse in-depth jumps, 82-83
 scoop tosses, 88-89
 split squat jumps, 64-65
 split squat walk, 60-61
 squat jumps, 67
 standing broad jump, 68-69
 upper body exercises, 84-95

 warm-ups, 57, 58
power eating, myth of, 14-17
power skipping, 75
progressive resistance, 8, 10
protein, dietary, 14, 15
protein supplements, 14
push-ups
 with chairs, 22
 in circuit training, 123-125, 132-137
 crab, 124-123, 137
 diamond, 134
 increasing resistance, 10
 inward-grip, 23
 knee, 23
 piked, 136
 strength assessment with, 13
 wide-grip, 134-135

**Q**uad stretches, 102

**R**epetitions
 in calisthenics, 20
 in circuit training, 98
resistance
 control of, 8-10
 progressive, 8, 10
reverse in-depth jumps, 82-83
rocker, 108-109
rope climbing circuit, 138-141
rowing, 126-127
 bent-over, 128
rung series, 118
running
 hill, 112-113
 stairs, 110

**S**andbag circuit, 128-131
scapular shrugs, 27
scoop tosses, 88-89
self-assessment, 12-13
shoulder strength assessment, 13
sissy squats, 116
sit-ups
 increasing resistance, 9

medicine ball, 92-93
 negative, 34-35
skipping, power, 75
spider, 102
split squat jumps, 64-65
split squat walk, 60-61
squat jumps, 67
 split, 64-65
squats
 demi, 51
 full, 52-53
 sissy, 116
squat walk, split, 60-61
stair circuit, 110-111
standing broad jump, 68-69
straight crunches, 106-107
stretches, 100-103

**T**high lifts
 diagonal, 43
 inner, 41
 outer, 45-47
thigh strength assessment, 13
toe touches, diagonal, 126-127
total body crunches, 36-37
triangle lifts, 39
triangle presses, 39
triceps lifts, 131
tuck jumps, double-leg, 62-63
twistie crunches, 106-107
twists, diagonal, 94-95
two-leg jumps, 111

**U**pper body exercises
 calisthenics, 22-27
 plyometrics, 84-95
upper body strength assessment, 13

**W**arm-ups, 12
 for calisthenics, 21
 for circuit training, 100-103
 for plyometrics, 57, 58
weight training, 8
wide-grip push-ups, 134-135